Changing School Culture For Black Males

Dr. Jawanza Kunjufu

Front cover illustration by Damon Stanford

First Edition, First Printing

Printed in the United States of America

ISBN #: 1-934155-82-9
ISBN #: 978-1-934155-82-0

DEDICATION

This book is dedicated to three Black males in eighth grade. Their names are Tyrone, Antoine, and Jamaal. They have similarities and differences. Tyrone's mother is a drug user and is being reared by his grandmother. They are poor and he attends an inner city school which is 100 percent African American. His major challenge is trying to avoid gangs and not being shot. There have been over 400 murders in his city this year. Antoine is being raised by a single, college-educated mother. He attends a charter school in a working class neighborhood. The school is equally divided between African Americans, Hispanics, and Whites. Jamaal lives in an affluent suburb with both parents. Only 10 percent of the students are African Americans. What they all have in common is they read at the sixth-grade level. They have been retained once. They have spent some time in special education classrooms and they have been suspended at least once.

Contents

Contents

Preface: The Most Important Question Facing Black Males

Educators, how would you answer that question? What would your Black male students say? What does the mass media promote? Which answer will give you a greater chance of securing a grant? Which answer creates more fear and anxiety?

The truth is that despite the educational crisis facing Black males, more Black males are going to college than prison:

- Black males in college – 1,400,000
- Black males in prison in – 841,000[1]

Let that sink in. Yes, 841,000 Black males in prison are too many. One Black male in prison is too many. However, despite their abysmal GPAs, low scores on state and national exams, referrals to special education and remedial reading, suspensions, and high dropout rates, more Black males are in college than in prison. This is a testimony to their innate brilliance, and I thank God every day that the school system has not and cannot destroy them. Our boys don't even know how gifted and blessed they truly are. We must convince them that they have a greater chance of going to college than prison.

All my questions, research, and consulting experiences have led me to an inescapable conclusion: We must change school culture to help *all* children reach their fullest potential, and the group that would benefit the most from a new school culture would be Black boys. As this book, *Changing School Culture for Black Males,* unapologetically advances, our boys deserve the same attention to their holistic development that other students receive.

Let the cultural transformation of schools begin with truth and faith, not lies and fear.

Introduction: What Black Males Need to Be Taught

Educators, do you like Black boys? Do you respect Black boys? Do you bond with Black boys?

Have you ever asked Black boys if they like attending your school? What do they like about being in your school? What do they dislike about your school?

Is your school fair to Black boys? Are the rules enforced fairly across race and gender?

How many boys in your school have had their spirits broken? This is an important question. How do we assess and measure the degree to which a boy's spirit has been broken? How are the spirits of Black boys being broken? How do we begin the process of repairing and restoring the spirits of Black boys?

Every time I see a Black boy standing in the corner of a classroom, I cringe. When I see a Black boy standing outside the classroom door, I wonder if the teacher could have found a better way to deal with the boy's behavior. When I see Black boys waiting in the principal's office, I know there's a better way, but I wonder if educators simply lack the will to try.

In workshops, I tell my audiences to go visit a kindergarten class and observe Black boys. These boys are eager, they sit in front of the class, they're on task. They love learning in kindergarten. Now visit a ninth-grade class. The boys are no longer sitting in the front. They're now sitting in the back of the class. They're sleeping, they're distracted, and some are disruptive. No longer are they asking questions or staying on task.

Something happens to our boys between kindergarten and ninth grade. I believe the three critical grades for Black boys are kindergarten, fourth grade, and ninth grade. Of those, the most critical is fourth grade, and I'll explain why later in this book.

What happens to Black boys' spirits between kindergarten and ninth grade? When a boy's spirit has been broken, can it ever be healed? How can schools prevent the spirits of Black boys from being broken?

This book will take a critical look at the spirits of our boys. We'll discuss what we can do to maintain their high level of enthusiasm in kindergarten and how to avoid their low spirit level in ninth grade.

This problem is much deeper than closing the racial academic achievement gap. We must close the relationship gap between Black boys and educators. But it goes even deeper than that. Try teaching a student with low self-esteem. Too many Black male students have low self-esteem. Later, in the book we will make a distinction between self and school esteem. What are schools doing to deflate the self-esteem of Black boys? Self-esteem is inextricably linked to spirit. If boys' spirits are broken, their self-esteem will be low. Unfortunately, this is a chronic, consistent problem I've seen in schools from Harlem to Compton. This book will look at what educators, administrators, and parents can do to enhance the self-esteem of African American boys.

My company, African American Images, publishes a curriculum called SETCLAE (Self-Esteem Through Culture Leads to Academic Excellence). There's a direct correlation between self-esteem and academic achievement. What's more, we've found that school culture is a key factor that influences self-esteem and academic achievement. School culture is the glue and the conduit through which boys will fail or succeed.

School Culture

So what is school culture? Every scholar will have his or her own definition, but I believe it is simply the matrix of values, norms, curriculum, pedagogy, classroom management, leadership styles of educators and the principal, and overall behaviors (of educators, administrators, staff, students, and parents) that characterize the vision, daily teaching and learning, and socialization of the school family. School culture conveys a certain feeling that can be detected the moment you walk through the doors. It communicates a message and quality of life and learning, and it powerfully influences all who work or attend as students.

For example, if your school has a positive "school spirit," this is a defining aspect of your school's culture, and it will influence educators and students to strive toward effective teaching and academic achievement. On the other hand, if your school décor is marked by metal detectors and your school day by random locker raids, this too gives personality to your school's culture and will motivate all who enter to operate in fear and suspicion. And let me just say that it is difficult to teach and learn in a culture of fear.

Interfacing with school culture is *youth culture.* African American youth culture is a response to hundreds of years of slavery, oppression, discrimination, racism, poverty and injustice. It is dynamic, fluid, highly creative, energetic, antagonistic against authority, and a powerful influence on its members. In recent years, hip hop has had the most

Introduction: What Black Males Need to Be Taught

influence on African American youth culture, and other races' youth as well.

Many believe the negative rhymes and images in rap songs and music videos have caused young people to adopt certain attitudes and behaviors that have negatively impacted their performance in school. However, rap is just one cultural pit stop in a long journey of consciousness raising and counterproductive thinking, fighting the power and integrating with it, that began when African Americans arrived on American shores for the second time in chains. Africans first arrived 800 BC. long before Columbus and built the Olmec civilization which included pyramids in Mexico. For example, in virtually all of my books, I talk about the widespread, destructive belief among African American youth that being smart is acting White and/or feminine. This idea originated decades before the innovation of hip hop, so we can't blame rap, although rap picked up the baton and ran with it, so to speak.

Imagine a Black boy loving math, but because he can't be seen as "White acting" or different from his peers, he deliberately sabotages himself. He doesn't turn in homework, and he refuses to study for an important test and does want to be recommended for Gifted or AP classes.It is very difficult for Black males to do well in school if their peers think being smart is feminine. It is difficult to do well if sports are valued over science, music over math, and rap over reading.

The Long Walk Home

Black boys face a major challenge that is seldom considered relevant to academic performance. This challenge has nothing to do with algebra, geometry, or trigonometry, biology, chemistry, or physics. For many Black boys, their greatest challenge is the walk from home to school and back, trying to avoid gangs and violence. Does your school provide any resources to protect Black boys during their daily transportation to and from school?

Ideally, schools should provide the resources students will need, such as security, to live a better life in their communities. In addition to security, the curriculum should provide the practical lessons our boys need to survive and thrive. I'm always amazed at the tremendous disconnect between the curriculum, which in America is primarily Eurocentric, and the needs of our boys. If you ask Black boys to talk about their major challenges and concerns and then review the curriculum they must digest, the disconnect becomes glaringly apparent.

I'm surprised the national dropout rate isn't more than 50 percent—unfortunately, in some cities it is.

Another stop on the long walk home is home itself. Our boys are angry for a myriad of reasons. For 72 percent of African American children, fathers are not in the home.[3] Too many of our boys have never even seen their fathers or have had only limited interactions with them. As a result, they toggle between anger and denial. When you see a Black male student playing it cool, he may be in denial about how fatherlessness has led to feelings of sorrow and depression. No male in his sphere of influence, whether in his neighborhood or in the media or greater society, has shown him how to process such overwhelming feelings, so he becomes oppositional. It is very difficult teaching a boy who is angry yet desperately wants to be nurtured and given direction by his father who might be incarcerated, on drugs, in a gang, dead, or simply AWOL. It is unfortunate that I have to ask schools to at least consider the impact this has on their students' academic performance and classroom behavior. However, it is better to proactively address fatherlessness than ignore it; otherwise, it will appear as anger and defiance in the cafeteria, gymnasium, classroom, or on the playground. The goal is to prevent disciplinary issues and wholesale withdrawal from the academic experience.

I am reminded of the biblical Scripture where God says, "This is my beloved Son, in whom I am well pleased" (Matthew 3:17). A boy wants or needs nothing more than for his father to tell him he is pleased with him. Unfortunately, too many of our boys will never hear those words from their fathers.

To add to this sad state of affairs, in many schools there is not one Black man in the building. And if a man is there, I'm willing to wager he's a custodian first, security guard second, P.E. teacher third, administrator fourth, and a classroom teacher last.

Many African American boys have never had a Black male teacher, and if they did have one, it was after fourth grade. Their first male teacher might not have been until seventh, eighth, or ninth grade. That may be too late.

If we want to change the culture for Black boys, if we want to make the environment more engaging for them, we must improve their relationships with the adults in the building. We must do whatever it takes to enhance their self-esteem. That includes addressing fatherlessness and their fear of gangs and violence as they go to and from school.

Introduction: What Black Males Need to Be Taught

We must address their sense of hopelessness and fatalism about their futures. It is very difficult to teach a child who does not see himself in the future. If you don't believe you're going to see your 18th birthday, then there is no need to stay in high school until you're 18. We must convince Black boys that they will live beyond 80 years of age. We have to teach them how to do that.

One thing I know about the male ego is that if a male doesn't believe he's going to be successful, he will withdraw. It doesn't take a Black boy long to decide whether he is going to be successful in school. It's a wonder some stay in school as long as they do.

Education is about long-term gratification. If you give a young person nine years of elementary school (K–8), four years of high school, four years of college, and possibly two to four years of graduate school, the promise and expectation is that you will have at least a middle-income lifestyle. But if you're an African American male who, in the primary grades, is being placed in the corner and referred to the lowest reading group, you might begin to feel quite hopeless.

Tracking begins much earlier than in the upper grades with student referrals to AP and honors classes. Tracking begins as early as kindergarten when the teacher divides the students into three reading groups: Eagles, Bluebirds, and Robins. It doesn't take long for Black boys to realize they are in the lowest reading group in kindergarten and first grade and that when they have to read aloud, the other students read better than they do. When they see the failing grades on their report cards, when they are held back a grade, when they are called dummies and mentally retarded by their peers because they have to take special education classes, it doesn't take long for them to give up on school. When they spend more time out of school on suspension than in school learning, they have begun their withdrawal from the academic experience.

Unfortunately, some state governors understand only too well how poor school performance, specifically fourth-grade reading scores, determine prison growth. Are we sending our boys to college, or are we sending them to prison?

Looking at schools historically and the end result of educational policy in this country today, I can't help but think that schools were never designed to educate all children. Could it be that schools are actually successful? Schools are designed to mirror our economy, to mirror classism. If schools were 100 percent successful and all students were earning A's and scoring 1600 or better on the SAT, then who would make up the unemployed and underemployed? Capitalism needs a certain number of unemployed people to drive wages down. If everyone were employed, then employers would have to raise wages. If schools were successful and everyone earned straight A's and were in the 99th percentile of national tests, who would work at McDonald's and Walmart? Who would clean up the schools at night? Who would populate prisons? Let's be honest about this. School culture is designed to produce winners and losers. As we understand that, then we can see how schools have been very successful.

Unfortunately, an unacceptable number of African American males are losing. It's true, there are more Black males in college than in prison, but there are still too many Black males in prison! African American males are almost 13 percent of the adult male population in America, yet they are 40.1 percent of the male prison population. Nationwide, African American youth represent 58 percent of youth admitted to state prisons.[4] Is there really a school-to-jailhouse pipeline? Could prisons remain in existence without African American males? Are prisons dependent on schools miseducating Black boys in order for them to thrive?

What type of culture is most conducive for the development of African American males? What type of school environment produces African American males who pursue STEM—science, technology, engineering, and medicine? These are the primary questions of this book that I will attempt to answer in the following chapters.

In my book, *There is Nothing Wrong with Black Students*, I identified over 3,000 schools in low-income, single-parent Black and Latino neighborhoods where Black and Latino students rank well above the national average. Some schools are succeeding. This book looks specifically at what we can do for African American male students.

The first thing we must do is change the mind-set of educators. Many believe that if a Black child is from a low-income, single-parent home where the parent lacks a college degree, he will not be academically successful. If we don't do anything else, we must change that mind-set.

As I document in the chapter on school culture, it is not the race, income, gender, or educational background of the parent that matters— it is the belief among the staff that they can produce students of excellence regardless of the social demographics. That is the first step we must address in improving school culture. How do we do that?

The major player in the educational arena is the principal. He/she is, or should be, the coach of the school. In sports it is no accident that some

Introduction: What Black Males Need to Be Taught

coaches move from one team to another and everywhere they go, they create winning teams. They change the culture of the team. The coach convinces the players that they can win. The problem for Black boys is that they attend schools where leadership is inconsistent. In some schools, students have had four principals in four years and the school remains ineffective, its culture unchanged.

The Wallace Foundation document in their research, the impact principals have on test scores. In middle-income schools, there is a 10 percent variance in test scores depending on the quality of the principal. In more challenging schools, the variance widens to 20 percent. A highly effective principal can raise test scores by 20 percent or more in Black, low-income, single-parent neighborhoods.[5]

It takes time to improve school culture. It cannot be changed in one year. School culture will stagnate if the principal's door is a revolving one—four principals in four years. When such chronic attrition is occurring, the root of the problem goes beyond the principal. We are now looking at the superintendent and the school board of the entire district. No effective superintendent or school board would allow a school to operate under those conditions of uncertainty year after year.

Another problem is that some principals spend most of the school day in their offices. They seldom walk the corridors. They only observe teachers once a year during evaluation time. They do not know most of the students. They have poor relationships with parents, and they've done little outreach to community organizations, churches, and businesses.

There are two types of principals: CEOs and instructional leaders. CEOs love their offices. They believe they are the accountant of the school and the manager of the physical resources. They spend the bulk of their day in their offices. The average principal spends less than 20% of their day as an instructional leader. Many principals have not taught a class since they became a principal. I believe you can evaluate a teacher better if you spend more time as an instructional leader and when you actually teach a class. I am even more concerned when over 80% of teachers receive an excellent evaluation from someone who spends so little time in that capacity. In addition, how can so many teachers receive such stellar evaluations when only 12% of Black boys are proficient in reading by 8th grade? Instructional leaders arrive early and stay late to both meet their management responsibilities and oversee learning in the school. During each and every school day they take the time to walk the corridors, talk to students, observe teachers in action, and establish relationships with parents, community organizations, businesses, and churches.

I'm always looking for solutions and I never give up. If there is an educator reading this book who is in a school where principal turnover is high or the principal is an ineffective leader, I encourage you to ask your principal to read this book. I offer a wealth of strategies that principals can begin to implement in their schools today. Some of the ideas, such as looping and single-gender male classrooms, will take time to implement, but there's no reason you can't begin planning today. The situation is just that urgent for Black boys.

In this book I will refer often to the following mantra: 20-*25 students, three/four years at a time*. If you can't save all Black boys, then determine to make a difference in the lives of 20-25 Black boys for three/ four years at a time. Start where you can. For example, have one teacher work with 20- 25 Black boys from kindergarten to second grade. This is looping. At the junior and senior high school level, students would have the same language arts teacher for four years, the same math teacher for four years, the same social studies teacher for four years, the same science teacher for four years, the same P.E. teacher for four years. We want to save 20-25 Black boys at a time every three/four years.

I do not want to get into a debate with the organization Teach for America. I am pleased with the energy, talent, and commitment of these young students who have signed up with Teach for America, but I think it's unfortunate that the commitment is only for two years. People can say what they want about this program. More than 70 percent of the students in Teach for America leave after two years. It is an excellent program, but the problem is the two-year commitment. In schools where the principal attrition rate is the highest, some of the best teachers in the building are leaving every two years. It is very difficult to improve school culture under these conditions.

When you look at the success of KIPP, the Knowledge Is Power Program, and the 3,000 plus schools that I identified in *There's Nothing Wrong with Black Students*, the principals and teachers of these schools go well beyond the call of duty. There's a sense of urgency in those schools. Later, I'll discuss how successful schools have a mission statement, a creed that they live by, and a commitment to stay and see the job through for the sake of their students.

Many teachers, especially White female teachers, are surprised to find themselves in low-income, inner city school districts where the

Introduction: What Black Males Need to Be Taught

children have tremendous needs. They did not receive a plum position in White suburban school districts and feel cheated by the system. I understand that teaching from 9 to 3 is what they thought they were going to do, but these students need much more than a 9-to-3 approach to commitment.

Most teachers have been trained to teach the *Leave it to Beaver/ Father Knows Best* children. They've been taught to teach children whose parents will monitor and assist them with homework. They thought they would be teaching children who come to school motivated and with home training. They were not prepared for the state of emergency in low-income schools and communities. Educating African American children is a mission, a calling, a ministry. I accept the fact that not all teachers have signed up to do that. Many teachers have told me, "I have a life. I'm willing to teach from 9:00 until 3:00, but at 3:00 I want to go home to my spouse and children, take them to soccer practice, and do the hobbies that I enjoy around my house. I am not interested in arriving at 7 in the morning, leaving at 7 at night, giving children my cell phone number, talking to them throughout the evening about their homework, about their abusive parent, about the challenges in their neighborhood, and on and on and on."

I understand and I accept that. However, I will say this. What I will not accept is that between 9:00 and 3:00 you lower your expectations, have poor classroom management, refuse to offer differentiated instruction, don't appreciate children's unique learning styles, and assume because they are Black and from low-income, single-parent homes that they cannot learn.

Even teachers who lack a sense of mission around Black children can still be very successful if they refuse to embrace the cultural deficit model. Educators of successful schools do not believe in the cultural deficit model. They believe in the school empowerment model. They believe that their school culture will overcome any cultural deficits.

If you think that superintendents allowing new principals every year or allowing principals to hide out in their offices during most of the school day is acceptable, Houston, we really have a problem. If teachers do not believe they can make a difference in the lives of low-income children from single-parent homes, then what hope do our boys have for an exceptional education?

We must improve school culture. We must change the mind-set that the street has a greater influence on our children than we do.

The World of Black Boys

Should Black boys come into your world, or should you go into theirs? There is a tremendous disconnect between school culture and Black male culture. Too often teachers believe the school is "our world." This is our curriculum, our lesson plans, our pedagogy, our classroom, our décor.

The general attitude among educators is, "This is our world, and when you come into our school, these are the rules." It's *this* curriculum, it's *this* pedagogy, it's *this* test. We determine if you get recess, when you receive P.E., when you get to eat lunch. We determine all of it. We will not make adjustments based on your neighborhood, which may be plagued by gangs, fatherlessness, unemployment, crime, and other social ills. You came into *our* world.

What if, as an experiment, we wanted to come into the world of Black males? Suppose we asked Black boys the following questions:

- What would make you want to be at our school as early as possible and stay as late as you desire?
- What could we do to make your lives better?
- What could we do to give you better economic options other than sports, rap, or drugs?
- What could we do to create a gang truce to reduce the violence in your community?

These questions suggest that at least we're willing to try and understand their world. If we want to improve school culture, we must understand their world. I encourage educators to make home visits, talk to parents, walk the same streets your children must walk through. The brilliant educator and author of Pedagogy of the Oppressed, Paulo Freire said, "true education begins with the experiences of the people." We must give Black males a voice in their education.

As educators, begin to investigate the world of Black males they will find that the Black community is not monolithic. We are many communities. In some schools, African Americans are less than 10 percent of the population; in others, they are 100 percent.

After all is said and done, the buck stops with the leadership—principals in schools, superintendents and board members at the district level. Sometimes principals don't even fully understand what's going on in their own schools because they don't disaggregate test scores. To fully understand how Black male students are doing at your school, consider disaggregating student scores. A group average may look like the entire student body is in the upper quartile of state or national test scores. But

Introduction: What Black Males Need to Be Taught

when you disaggregate the scores, you'll find only 5 percent of African American males in the upper quartile. If we are serious about improving school culture, the first step is getting a read on what's truly going on quantitatively! Principals and all school leaders must have the backbone, tenacity, and fortitude to disaggregate the scores.

On the other hand, disaggregating the scores will not help if you refuse to disaggregate the solutions.

Over my career, schools and school districts have brought me in because their Black male students were underperforming. They knew they were underperforming, but because these students made up less than 50 percent of the student body, they were unwilling to allocate the necessary resources to solve the problem. Why should I speak to the entire student body when there are 100 to 200 African American males who need urgent attention? I have no problem speaking to the entire student body, but why won't you let me work with your African American male students first? You know the answer to that: racism.

Speaking of racism, if we want to empower African American males, then we must teach them how to recognize and overcome racism.

Whether the population is 5 percent African American male and only 200 students or 100 percent African American and 1,000 students, we can implement the strategy for 20- 25 students three/four years at a time.

Before we proceed to the next chapter, let's look at the strategies that will improve school culture and help Black boys reach their fullest potential:

1. Getting Black boys reading at grade level
2. Believing that being smart is Black and masculine
3. Using history and culture to overcome Post-Traumatic Slavery Disorder
4. Recognizing and overcoming racism
5. Understanding capitalism and overcoming poverty
6. Understanding anger management, conflict resolution, and how to walk away from a fight
7. Developing goals and plans
8. Understanding and maximizing time management
9. The importance of the selection of friends
10. The importance of a positive attitude
11. A balanced emphasis between sports/entertainment and academics
12. Avoiding gangs and violence
13. Forgiving their fathers

14.   What it takes to be a good father
15.   Avoiding STDs and AIDS
16.   Respecting authority, elders, and women
17.   Understanding the significance of choices and consequences
18.   Developing high self-esteem
19.   Understanding the impact of media on values
20.   Understanding the impact of illegal and legal drugs
21.   Avoiding incarceration
22.   Valuing education
23.   Thriving under the guidance of a male mentor
24.   The importance of a good work ethic
25.   Living to see their 80th birthday

Review the above 25 points. I encourage you to enlarge them into a poster and refer to them often. Share these points with other staff, parents and students. Does your curriculum address any of these issues? In my humble opinion, these are significant issues for African American males. If we want to empower them, these are the issues that need to be brought into schools to improve the culture for Black males.

This book is designed to provoke thought and jump-start change. You'll notice that many of the chapters are actually in questionnaire format. I encourage you and your colleagues to read through the questions and answer them as honestly as possible.

Chapter 1: Framework

In this chapter, I present a series of ideological statements and questions about the education of African American males and the challenges they face. The purpose of these ideas is to provoke thought, and I'll explore many of the ideas in the chapters that follow. These ideas lay the foundation for this book and support my thesis that if we are to help our boys achieve their fullest potential, we must change school culture.

- It is very difficult, if not impossible, to transform school culture without the leadership of the principal.

- It normally takes two to four years to change the culture in a school. One to three teachers can change the culture of a school positively or negatively.

- Some teachers believe they don't see color. They see children as children.

- Does your school have a zero tolerance policy? Restorative justice or grace?

- Do you teach the way you want to teach or do you teach the way your children learn?

- Is it cool for boys to be smart at your school?

- Gangs exist and thrive when fathers, male teachers and mentors are absent.

- No other group has a sports fixation like African American males. We must change the culture from sports to science, music to math, rap to reading.

- Are athletes and entertainers the only positive role models for African American males?

- Streets are dangerous when they are filled with young, illiterate, fatherless, unemployed Black males who lack goals and morals and have plenty of guns.

- Single-gender schools are not a panacea. They cannot be effective with CEO principals, incompetent teachers who have low expectations of their students, poor classroom management skills, and do not offer an adequate amount of time on task.

- Schools must change the culture that being smart is acting White and feminine.

Chapter 1: Framework

- Schools must make scholarship Africentric and masculine.

- Teachers cannot allow one to three students to negatively change the culture of the classroom.

- Do teachers know how to convert a class clown or thug to a scholar?

- There is no such person as a bad boy.

- Do some schools and teachers take away gym and recess as a form of punishment?

- Do schools understand that males are warriors?

- Do Black boys view out of school suspension as a vacation?

- Boys are not afraid of prison. It has become their rite of passage.

- Does your school dislike Black boys?

- Do you like Black boys?

- Which teachers in your school have a poor relationship with Black males?

- Which teachers have an excellent relationship with Black males?

- Do your males have a greater street IQ than school IQ?

- Could you survive their streets?

- We must expose Black males to Algebra before 9th grade.

- In your school, do girls give more respect to athletes or scholars?

- Why do some schools suspend Black males less than others?

- Suspensions increase with poor classroom management.

- Every Black male needs a positive adult role model.

- What could you do to make your school more attractive to Black males?

- Are gangster rappers raising Black boys?

- Black males are very competitive, but they work best in cooperative learning groups.

- What do Black males like about your school? What do they hate about your school?

- It's hard for most Black males to straddle the fence between school culture and Black male culture.

Chapter 1: Framework

- How many Black male scholars have we lost to the streets?

- Most Black males do not want to please their teacher.

- Most Black males do not snitch.

- The worst thing you can do to a Black male is call him a sissy.

- How difficult is it to develop a five-year-old Black male into a Ph.D in STEM (science, technology, engineering, or medicine)?

- Until Black boys understand White supremacy, everything else will confuse them.

- Most Black boys suffer from cultural amnesia.

- The first function of education is to give each child a positive identity.

- The difference between a low and high achieving school is simple.

- The high achieving school hasa mission of urgency that permeates throughout the building.

- In a positive school culture, educators are problem solvers. In a negative school culture, they are frustrated and complainers.

- Are there more Black students in prison or college?

- Every student everyday needs at least one meaningful interaction with an educator.

- Zero tolerance should not mean zero thought.

- Disengagement is different from defiance.

- If we do not close the achievement gap, we will permanently place African American students into a permanent underclass.

- If doctors have difficulty getting their sick patients to change their lifestyle, you can only imagine the challenges principals have changing the habits of their teachers.

- Fatherlessness is the precursor of illiteracy, special education, suspension, dropping out, drug addiction, gangs, crime, teen pregnancy, and incarceration.

- Only 28 percent of Black boys have their fathers in the home.

- What can schools do about fatherlessness?

- How many seventh- to 12th-grade males are fathers?

- What are the classroom implications of boys being angry at their absent father?

Chapter 1: Framework

- What are the classroom implications of being a mama's boy?

- What are the classroom implications of being told by your mother that you are the man of the house?

- The most influential factor for students is not family income or being raised by a single mother who lacks a college degree. *Conversation* in the home and teacher's lounge is the greatest influence.

- What is the classroom implication of video game addiction?

- Do boys have a short attention span when they play sports and video games?

- We must understand the male ego. It is large and fragile.

- Males thrive on success. They drop out or withdraw if they do not feel they have a chance to be successful.

- Does your school nurture or destroy the male ego?

- We must convince Black males that they will see their 80th birthday.

- Black males should not disengage from academics every year for three months of summer vacation.

- Twenty-eight percent of core academic teachers at predominately minority schools lack appropriate certifications.

- As age increases, so does the influence of peer pressure and street culture.

- Black males must be taught how to recognize and overcome racism.

- Every Black male needs a schedule and structure. Being on a sports team enhances self-esteem, reduces stress, teaches anger management, provides an adult mentor, teaches discipline, provides structure, and emphasizes teamwork.

- Every Black male must have a purpose in life.

- Do we have at-risk Black males or at-risk schools?

- The new form of discrimination is based on zip code.

- You are not at risk because you're Black, poor, and fatherless. You are at risk when you lack goals.

Chapter 1: Framework

- How can we live in a capitalistic society and not teach Black males capitalism?

- The majority of Black males hate school by the time they enter junior high.

- Have rap lyrics moved from "fight the power" to kill the N and B?

- How are gangsta rap lyrics affecting the male psyche?

- Black boys know that one mistake on the street could cost them their lives.

- Every Black male should take the chip off his shoulder and take responsibility for his life.

- Every Black male should receive anger management classes.

- We must convince Black males they can achieve their career goals.

- Poverty devalues academics. Have we taught Black males how to overcome poverty?

- What do you teach Black males in school who are involved in a gang war?

- Are schools preparing Black males to work in factories that no longer exist?

- Are schools preparing Black males to be inmates?

- Whose job is it to motivate Black males?

- Whose job is it to give Black males home training?

- How do we convince Black males to believe in long-term gratification?

- Do Black males believe the gun is the great equalizer?

- Single mothers can raise a boy without a man in *her* life but not in *his* life.

- What are the differences between school and street culture?

- Do some Black males believe doing homework is betraying the race and male culture?

- Do Black males believe they can get an A in algebra or chemistry without studying or doing homework?

- Do you know why Thursday is a better test day than Monday?

Chapter 1: Framework

- Do you know why May is a better test month than September?

- Are Black male athletes celebrated in your school and Black male scholars scorned? What can your school do better to reward Black male scholars?

- Black boys know by fourth grade whether school will be advantageous for them.

- Black boys want someone to teach them discipline.

- Black boys want teachers to care about them.

- Why don't more Black males become teachers? Why won't schools hire more Black males?

- Do schools have a hidden White middle-class curriculum?

- What are some best practices of Black male students that we can use in the classroom?

- The drive to be cool is a response to racism.

- Saggin' is a response to racism.

- The greatest problem facing Black males in school is not academics. It's the disconnect between school and street culture.

- Schools must create a culture of academic achievement.

- What can teachers learn from sports to make their classrooms more attractive to Black males?

- If most schools are resistant to disaggregating test scores by race and gender, then that explains why they are hesitant about providing solutions about race and gender.

- Boys are *different* from girls; they are not *deficient*.

- Black male culture must be integrated into schools. Can you imagine a school where the staff is 83 percent male? A school that rewards aggression by having students exercise the first five minutes of every hour? A school where the majority of the books are about sports, hip hop, science fiction, animals, male characters, and technology? A classroom with no chairs, tables have replaced desks and most classes are taught outside without textbooks, lectures and worksheets? Homework is only for 10 minutes?

Chapter 1: Framework

- Why would a Black male want to be in AP, honors, gifted & talented classes in your school?

- Why are so many Black males angry and have chips on their shoulders?

- The Latin definition of "education" means to draw forth from within. Education is not about training Black boys to be docile and take exams.

- Do your Black male students value fighting and sports over academics?

- Has your school taught Black males how to resolve conflict through nonviolence?

- Which is worse: a crumbling school, insensitive teachers, overcrowded classrooms, or student violence? Many African American students endure all of the above.

- Every Black male should experience a military boot camp.

- Black males make silly mistakes when they have nothing to lose, when they don't have goals.

- Why is it so difficult to teach Black males how to read? Is illiteracy the precursor for retention, special education, dropping out, and incarceration?

- Retention or social promotion? How does it feel to be a Black male in ninth grade, 16 years of age, with a fourth-grade reading score?

- Who in your school determines the selection of books to be read by Black males?

- What type of books do young Black males like to read?

- Do schools know how to teach young Black males how to write?

- How difficult is it for a principal to change the culture of a school when the majority of his/her staff has tenure?

- What is the pecking order among your students? How significant is the pecking order around academic achievement? What do you about the Alpha male theory?

Chapter 1: Framework

- When Black males wear saggin' pants, females wear revealing clothes, and teachers wear jeans, it says a lot about your school culture.

- We must teach Black males how to be strong mentally, not just physically.

- Many Black males want to succeed in school without studying or completing homework.

- Is there a cultural disconnect between some White female teachers and Black boys?

- Is there a cultural disconnect between some middle-class Black educators and low-income Black male students?

- Can you teach a child of whom you are afraid?

- Boys do not do well in school if they are not allowed to release their energy.

- There is a difference between self-esteem and school-esteem.

- Black males could be failing their classes but still have high self-esteem.

- Can Black males trust you as a teacher?

- Do you see your Black male students as future success stories?

- Teachers must have the attitude, "I refuse to let you fail or settle for mediocrity."

- There is a difference between "My students *will* learn" and "My students *can* learn."

- When teachers refer to a Black male student as *son*, they have begun the bonding process.

- If we want to change school culture, the best teachers should teach in the earlier grades.

- Black males view themselves as athletic stars. Some teachers view them as ignorant.

- There are no significant differences in dis-identification with academics by race or gender in primary grades. However, no group dis-identifies more with academics by ninth grade than Black males.

Chapter 1: Framework

- What do your Black male students do between 3:00 pm and 6:00 pm?

- How many Black males in your school have talents that go undeveloped?

- Why should Black males stay in your school if they are not learning anything that will help them survive the streets?

- In some school districts, students are arrested and handcuffed for talking back to teachers, possessing cell phones, or violating the dress code.

- Female behavior should not be the school standard. Boys have no desire to act like girls.

- We could reduce special education placements by reinstating recess, daily P.E., and allowing more movement in the classroom.

- More than any other factor, the percentage of Black males in special education and suspension reflects what you think of them.

- Some students are absent a lot and drop out of school because they have nothing to wear or don't like the clothes.

- We are not going to positively change school culture for Black males until we teach them how to overcome poverty and acquire wealth.

- It is difficult being a transformational teacher in a traditional school environment. The major catalyst for change is not funding, curriculum, school or class size, or whether the school is public, charter, or private. The major catalyst is a transformational school culture.

- In high achieving schools, classroom doors are open, and principals visit frequently.

- We must celebrate good teachers.

- While funding is important, it is not as important as relationship.

- In predominately minority schools, only 65 percent offer Algebra II; 40 percent offer physics, and only 29 percent offer calculus.

- Do we know how to teach oral learners, tactile learners, picture learners, and kinesthetic learners in intermediate, upper, and high school?

Chapter 1: Framework

- Primary-grade children do not lose their learning style in the upper grades. Most upper grade teachers simply do not meet the needs of right brain learners.

- A school can determine the future and destroy a boy's life by placing him in lower track classes.

- Have we designed schools and the calendar for adults or for students?

- It cost more to correct failure than to produce success.

- Pre-school is a much better investment than prison.

- How many minutes per day, week, month, and year do Black males in your school spend in the corner, outside the door, and in the principal's office?

- Programs are progress, but policy is power. Teachers implement programs. Administrators implement policy.

- Boys measure everything by one yardstick: Does this make me look weak?

- In some neighborhoods, the most important skill to learn for Black males is survival. I wonder how many teachers could survive the streets of their students?

- Hollering sit down and shut up is not good classroom management.

- Some teachers have replaced textbook and worksheets with boring lectures and videos.

- Master educators teach on their feet and not in their seat.

- Memorizing is not learning. We must develop independent learners and problem solvers.

- Social promotions must cease. We cannot allow students to enter high school with elementary grade skills.

- How can we prepare students for high stakes testing if teachers give 30 minute exams and the state gives 90 minute exams?

- A major hinderance to changing school culture is the difficulty to remove an ineffective teacher. On average, it will require 3-5 years of principal's documentation and over $100,000 in legal fees.

Chapter 1: Framework

- School culture, staff optimism and collaboration is more significant than social demographics.

- If schools do not change the culture nothing will change.If schools do not change the culture nothing will change.

- It is better to change school culture by encouragement, role modeling and providing research than by coercion.

- Ironically, some affluent White parents are delaying their son's entrance into kindergarten until age 6(they have had pre-school for over 5 years) while poor Black parents try to convince principals their almost 5 year-old son (who has never had pre-school) is ready for kindergarten.

- Some schools have a culture of either humiliating or excluding Black males.

- Do some schools place Black males in special education for financial reasons?

- Are some boys placed in special education because they suffer from "White female teachers are afraid of Black Boys Syndrome?" Should we give teachers Ritalin too?

- You cannot discipline a student until you bond with them.

- If teachers are still learning students will learn.

- Some classrooms remind me of cemetaries: line them in rows and keep them quiet.

I would like you to review and ponder the above. Throughout the book, we will review these thoughts. Let's now apply them to the next chapter on School Culture.

Chapter 2: School Culture

In this chapter, we'll look at school culture from a general perspective. This and the Framework chapter lay the foundation for the premise of this book, which is that improving school culture is the key to helping Black male students succeed academically.

I have found excellent research that reinforces how important school culture is to not just Black males but all children. If you believe that race, gender, family income, educational background of the parent, and school funding determine educational outcomes, I'd like you to carefully read about the following studies, described in *Changing Schools*.[6]

> "Dr. Charles Payne, who cites ongoing research from the Consortium of Chicago School Research, [found] that when the Consortium compared the 30 most highly rated schools in Chicago with 30 of the lowest performing ones, it discovered questions related to the quality of relationships— in particular, the level of trust and respect teachers have for one another were among the best predictors of school performance."

The second study comes from Ohio State University.

> "In contrast, teachers in high-performing schools believe that as individuals, and as a group, they are capable of improving student achievement, and they trust their colleagues to work as hard as they do to make it happen. Ohio State University researcher Wayne Hoy and his colleagues have coined a term, 'academic optimism' as a way to define the cultures of high-performing schools, which display three characteristics:
> 1. Press for academic achievement
> 2. Collective efficacy (i.e., a shared belief among teachers that they can help students succeed)
> 3. Faculty trust in parents and students.
>   "After surveying teachers in nearly 100 schools, Hoy and his colleagues determined that academic optimism was an even more powerful predictor of student achievement

than socio-economic status: In the same way individuals can develop learned helplessness, organizations can be seduced by pervasive pessimism. According to the pessimist view, voiced with a tired recognition, 'These kids can't learn. There's nothing I can do about it, so why worry about academic achievement.'... Academic optimism, in stark contrast, views teachers as capable, students as willing, parents as supportive, and the task as achievable."

The third study comes from Kent Peterson.

"In the article, 'Positive or Negative?' (*Journal of Staff Development,* Summer 2002), Peterson writes about exemplary school culture.... In that article, Peterson described a school culture as a set of norms, values, beliefs, ceremonies, stories and symbols that make up the persona of the school. Staff, students, principal, and community members are all seen as learners. The presence of a staff professional library symbolically communicates the importance of learning. [In this one particular school that Kent Peterson observed] the staff has amassed 4,000 professional books and 400 videotapes on effective teaching and other professional issues. In addition, the school hosts an academy for parents each year to help enhance parenting abilities. 'Staff members feel responsible for improving their own skills and knowledge to help students learn.'

"A toxic school culture blames students for lack of progress, discourages collaboration among staff. A positive school culture celebrates successes, emphasizes accomplishments and collaboration, and fosters a commitment to staff and student learning."

Which describes your school culture?

Listed below is a chart describing a low achieving school (pessimism) and a high achieving school (optimism).

Chapter 2: School Culture

THEME	LOW ACHIEVING/PESSIMISM	HIGH ACHIEVING/OPTIMISM
Culture	Denial	Admit, understand, appreciate
Principal	CEO	Instructional leader
Staff	Custodian/Referral Agent / Instructor	Master Teacher/Coach
Atmosphere	Disdain for students	Respect and love for students and adults
Classroom door	Closed	Open
Principal visits	Once	Frequently
Collaboration	None	Teamwork
Responsibility	None, blames external factors	Full responsibility
Literature	Cultural deficit model	Cultural strength
Students	"Those children"	"My sons/daughters"
Décor	Drab/Eurocentric	Colorful/inspirational/Africentric
Values	I	We/Nguzo Saba/Ma'at
Time	Arrives late and leaves early	Arrives early/stays late
Mission/creed	None	Recite, meditate, and believe daily
Parents	No relationship	Home visits, parents are volunteers, partnership encouraged
Policy	Zero tolerance	Grace/mercy/forgiveness
Attitude	Favoritism	Fairness
Research	Nonexistent	Full library with books, videos, and articles
Pedagogy	Left brain only: "This is the way I teach."	Whole brain: "I teach the way my children learn."
Attire	Staff dresses like students	Professional
Fourth quarter	Shut down	Accelerated
Expectations	Low/some can learn	High/all will learn
Goals	High school diploma at best	Majority college degree
Curriculum	Eurocentric	Africentric
Certified	72 percent	100 percent
Teacher performance	Ignored	Celebrated
School tracking	AP/gifted and talented /special education/remedial	One school, no tracking
Motivation	"Not in my job description."	"Whatever it takes."
Teachers' lounge	Unrefuted, negative comments	Positive comments

I'd like my readers to review this chart and honestly ask yourselves if your school is low achieving and filled with pessimism, or is it a high achieving school and filled with optimism? Let's review some of the factors.

I often hear the statement, "I don't see color. I see children as children." I believe those teachers see culture and color better than anyone else. They see it so well they are in a state of denial. To be an effective teacher and to have a school culture that maximizes students, you need to admit that race and culture are factors. That's the first step.

The second step is to understand and read about the culture of your students. Large numbers of White female teachers grew up in rural and suburban neighborhoods, yet they're now teaching inner city Black and Hispanic students. Unfortunately, while students in college, many were not given the proper preparation to teach these students. The first step is to admit that race and culture are factors. The second step is to understand race and culture. The third step is to appreciate the culture.

Where are you? In a state of denial? Do you admit that race and culture are important? Do you understand the culture of your Black male students? How did you do on those earlier quizzes in the book? Do you appreciate culture?

Which Type of Teacher Are You?
There are five types of teachers:
1. Custodians
2. Referral Agents
3. Instructors
4. Master Teachers
5. Coaches

Custodians say, "I have mine and you have yours to get. Shut up and sit down. They graduated from college 30 years ago and are using the same lesson plans 30 years later.

Referral Agents have a high propensity to send children to special education and the principal's office for suspension. Research shows 20 percent of the teachers make almost 80 percent of the referrals into special education.

Instructors believe they teach subjects, not students. They believe they teach algebra and chemistry, not students. They never adjust their pedagogy or bond with students. They believe that subject matter is most important. Unfortunately, from the fourth grade on, we have more Instructors, which contributes to the fourth-grade syndrome and the decline in performance among African American students.

Master Teachers not only understand subject matter like Instructors, they also understand pedagogy. They know that there must be congruence between pedagogy and learning styles. You don't teach the way you want to teach. You teach the way your children learn.

Coaches understand subject matter and pedagogy. They also understand that you cannot teach a child you do not like, respect, or understand. Master teachers and coaches are always learning. They learn from their students. Their students teach them the best pedagogy to use. Their students teach them how to bond, encourage, challenge and discipline. They are constantly reading articles and books in their field. Can you imagine a doctor refusing to heal sick patients? The doctor has decided to only treat healthy patients. Custodians, referral agents and teachers have decided to only work with motivated students who have good home training, who share their values and are academically on grade level. They have decided their job is to "cover the material" and not teach the child. They are not even cognizant that the statements are diabolical. Master teachers and coaches have a mantra: I refuse to let you fail.

The struggle on who shapes school culture is first determined by the principal. Second, the struggle is between master teachers/coaches vs. custodians/referral agents and instructors. The former is usually smaller, less vocal and chooses to avoid the teacher's lounge. As a result, the latter oftentimes wins by default. My major concern is that with a 50% teacher turnover every five years, we are constantly receiving new teachers who are being influenced more by the latter and CEO principals. If we are going to successfully change school culture, we need master teachers /coaches and principals who are instructional leaders to be more vocal, take back the teacher's lounge and aggressively go after new teachers as soon as they arrive.

You can tell an awful lot about a teacher based on whether the classroom door is open or closed. You can tell a lot about a principal based on whether they make one annual visit to classrooms for the sole purpose of evaluation or whether they visit frequently and there is dialogue and interaction with teachers.

Low achieving schools are filled with pessimism, and teachers really believe they can close their door and do whatever they want with their students. They know the principal is not scheduled for the annual visit until another date, and they know they're not being monitored.

High achieving schools filled with optimism have an open-door policy. Not only are principals walking in and out of classrooms, observing teachers, but many times, teachers are walking in and out of each other's classrooms, observing one another. Principals are teaching classes and allowing the less effective teacher to observe the master teacher.

In the research mentioned above, collaboration was cited as very important. In low achieving schools, there is very little collaboration. You'll have a Master Teacher in Room 201 and a new, ineffective teacher in room 203, teaching the same grade. Because of the closed-door policy and lack of collaboration, the ineffective teacher seldom if ever gets a chance to observe the Master Teacher. The high achieving school filled with optimism has an open-door policy, and the new teacher is encouraged to observe the Master Teacher. This teamwork that takes place in high achieving schools contributes to their success.

Literature

Low achieving schools filled with pessimism subscribe to the cultural deficit model. They believe there's something wrong with the children. The children are broken. There's nothing wrong with the staff. There's nothing wrong with the school.

High achieving schools filled with optimism don't believe in the cultural deficit model. They believe in their students' cultural strengths. They have found data that there are thousands of schools in Black, Hispanic, low-income, single parent, drug and gang infested neighborhoods, where parents lack college degrees and are not involved in their children's education ,but the schools have their students well above the national average. They are problem solvers and not complainers. They understand that children who listen to rap lyrics and in minutes can repeat the words verbatim can also master reading, math, and science. They appreciate the energy level of their students. They understand and appreciate the history and culture of their students.

Décor

I can tell a lot about a classroom by the décor of the facility. In low achieving schools filled with pessimism, the décor is so drab that live children die in those schools. Unfortunately, after the primary grades, many intermediate and upper-grade teachers do not feel the need to provide inspirational décor for their students. I can't tell you how many schools I visited before the election of President Barack Obama where the school is all African American and yet, the main corridor is filled with pictures of mostly dead White male presidents. What you put on the walls of your classroom and school tells me more than anything what you think of African American students. Remember the teacher who told me she did not see color? When I visited her class, I observed an all white bulletin board for all Black students! What do boys see when they enter your class? Do they see themselves? Are they empowered?

Chapter 2: School Culture

Time

When the bell rings at the end of the day, the faculty at low achieving schools filled with pessimism often leaves the building faster than the students. In contrast, in high achieving schools filled with optimism, teachers arrive early. They discuss lesson plans with each other. They share articles and books and watch instructional videos together. When the students leave at the end of the day, the faculty remains and continues a high level of collaboration. In low achieving schools, time is lost due to intercom and telephone usage. In high achieving schools the above is highly monitored or eliminated.

Mission Statement

Does your school have a mission statement or creed? How visible is the statement? Unfortunately, in low achieving schools filled with pessimism, there is no mission statement. But in high achieving schools filled with optimism, not only is there a mission statement, it is in every classroom and every corridor, in the cafeteria, gymnasium, and auditorium. Not only is it visible, it is recited, meditated upon, and internalized daily.

Policy

Low achieving schools filled with pessimism have a zero tolerance policy. If a student makes one mistake, the police may be called. The student will be handcuffed and driven away to the police station. In high achieving schools filled with optimism, students receive a second, third, and fourth chance. These schools are filled with grace, mercy, and forgiveness.

In zero tolerance schools, discipline is administered based on favoritism. In high achieving schools, children are disciplined fairly across the board. Children, especially African American children who already believe that racism exists, are concerned about teachers and administrators treating them unfairly. In high achieving schools, educators make students feel safe.

Attire

In some schools there's little difference between how teachers and students dress. In low achieving schools, you'll see teachers dressing more casually than the students. In high achieving schools filled with optimism, teachers dress like role models. They raise the bar for students. They give students a clear image of what they expect them to look and dress like in the future.

The Fourth Quarter

In low achieving schools filled with pessimism, the teachers are already packing up their books and supplies during the last few weeks of the school year. Little learning is going on. They are waiting for summer vacation to begin.

In high achieving schools, teachers understand that the most important quarter is the fourth quarter. Just like in basketball and football, you don't win based on the score at the end of the third quarter. You win based on the final score at the end of the fourth quarter. Students at low achieving schools would perform much better if teachers taught with the same zeal in the fourth quarter as they did in the first quarter.

You can tell an awful lot about a school, its leadership and faculty by how much learning is going on during the last quarter, the last month, the last week, and the last day.

Goals

Unfortunately, in low achieving schools filled with pessimism, teachers believe that a good year is when 50 percent of their students improved. In high achieving schools they believe all students improved.

If you don't believe your students are going to do well, this belief will affect how you design your lesson plan and your pedagogy, and it will affect how you relate to students. Students respond positively to teachers who believe in them, who refuse to give up on them. You have to be convinced of the outcome before you invest in the practice.

Curriculum

Low achieving schools use a Eurocentric curriculum with African American students. High achieving schools use an Africentric curriculum with their African American students. Did Columbus really discover America? Did Abraham Lincoln really free the slaves? Is Hippocrates really the father of medicine?

You can tell a lot about a school based on what they teach about Egypt and slavery. Some schools have actually taken Egypt out of Africa and placed it in the Middle East. They never inform their African American students that Africans, not Romans, not Greeks, built the pyramids and developed the laws of math and science.

Chapter 2: School Culture

Some schools devote about a paragraph to slavery. They teach more about the years after 1620 rather than the massive civilizations that Africans were engaged in building centuries before. It has always amazed me that in America, we know more about the Holocaust that took place in Germany than what happened during slavery right here in America. We know how many Jews died in Germany, but not how many Africans died in America during the slave trade.

What does your school teach about African and African American history?

Qualifications

Can you imagine affluent suburban parents allowing an art teacher to teach algebra, geometry, trigonometry, or calculus, or a math teacher to teach art? Can you imagine a high achieving principal allowing a music teacher to teach biology, chemistry, or physics, or a science teacher to teach music? In low achieving schools filled with pessimism, 28% of the teachers are not certified to teach their subjects. In high achieving schools filled with optimism, this is unacceptable.

Teacher Performance

In low achieving schools, a teacher who has produced a high achieving class is often shunned, ridiculed, and envied. In high achieving schools, these teachers are celebrated and encouraged. They inspire other teachers to do well. One of the most important components of an optimistic school culture is the rewarding of teachers' high level of performance.

We talk a lot about Black students being teased for doing well in school and being accused of acting White. Unfortunately, many teachers in low achieving schools experience the same thing. They are shown disdain for "showing up the other faculty." In Black, low-income, single-parent communities where many parents lack a college degree, many teachers are producing students who perform well above the national average. Too often these teachers are ignored. It's as if the rest of the faculty wants these brilliant teachers to dumb it down, lower the standards and expectations. In order to positively change school culture we must celebrate the success of teachers. I recommend a teacher of the month award. The criteria can either be quality of lesson plans, test performance, classroom management or some other indicator. The decision should be determined by a committee of teachers and administrators. The award should be special. One of the reasons for the success in Finland and Japan is that teachers review each other's lesson plans and they observe one another. In order to positively change school culture we must increase collaboration. I also recommend staff meetings rotate from classroom to classroom. Staff members with drab classrooms need to observe invigorating classrooms and they need to be embarrassed and hopefully challenged when the meeting is in their room. Last, we must make it uncomfortable for custodians, referral agents, and instructors. We must observe their classes regularly and have them observe master teachers. We must create an environment where they will either improve or request a transfer.

I am often asked by discouraged teachers how do you positively change school culture in a negative environment? I believe with good communication, sound data research, encouragement and strict monitoring. I share with them the response from fellow teachers. They have told me how frustrating it was to work 6 plus hours in a negative environment and not see positive results and how rewarding it is to work 7 plus hours in a positive school culture and observe positive results. Positively changing school culture is the best way to retain staff and avoid teacher turnover.

TRACKING/EXPECTATIONS

In low achieving schools filled with pessimism, tracking is implemented from kindergarten. A parent once told me that the tracking was so pronounced at her child's school that the regular students had classes on the first floor, and the advanced students were on the second floor. Seldom did the first and second floor students and staff interact with one another. In high achieving schools, AP, honors, gifted and talented classes are open to all students. Another parent told me how difficult it was to have his son placed in AP classes. The principal did not think he was ready and the teacher said she would not assist his son for the entire year. She made him feel unwelcomed the entire year. He earned an A in spite of the teacher. That is not the type of culture Black males need.

In low achieving schools, they lower expectations based on race, income, gender and appearance. In high achieving schools, they believe all students will learn because of their expectations. They believe if the child has not learned, the teacher has not taught.

Chapter 2: School Culture

Motivation

Teachers at low achieving schools filled with pessimism don't believe motivating students is in their job description. They believe that students should come already motivated. Parents should motivate their own children.

In high achieving schools filled with optimism, teachers have a motto: "Whatever it takes." If the student lacks home training, we'll give it to him. If the student lacks motivation, we'll give it to him. If the student's not finishing his homework, we'll help him get it done at school. The best way to motivate a student is to instill confidence in their strengths and make the curriculum relevant.

Teacher's Lounge

You can tell an awful lot about a school by the conversation in the teacher's lounge. It's a shame how some teachers talk about their students and parents. Even if you do not personally participate in these negative discussions, if you're not part of the solution, you're part of the problem. In low achieving schools filled with pessimism, the teachers know they can say whatever they want about African American students, and they will never be refuted or challenged. If the conversation in the teacher's lounge is not uplifting or about solving problems, then you should challenge the negativity.

In high achieving schools filled with optimism, you seldom if ever hear derogatory comments about students and their parents. If a derogatory comment is made, the teacher will be challenged. Principals who are instructional leaders must take back the lounge in order to change school culture. First, you must sit in the lounge when the staff is present. Second, you must provide books, articles and videos of successful schools in low-income areas. Last, you must steer the conversation away from complaints to solutions.

Urgency

In high achieving schools filled with optimism, there's a sense of urgency that extends from the teacher's lounge to the classroom. A sense of passion permeates throughout the building. Teachers are confident they can make a difference in the lives of their students. The culture of optimistic schools is intentional and infuses every segment, tool, and process of the school day. School culture is the most important factor that determines whether students are successful academically or not. It's not about resources. It's about relationships. It's not about charter schools versus regular schools. You could have a charter school with a low achieving, pessimistic culture. You could have a regular school that's high achieving and optimistic.

Bill Gates discovered that although class size is important, this is not the most important factor in academic success. If low achievement is infused in the culture of the school, it doesn't matter if there are 15 students in a class or 200 students in the school. Regardless of class or school size, low achieving, pessimistic cultures are ineffective. On the other hand, a class with 35 students or a school with 4,000 students can succeed if there is a culture of high achievement and optimism.

Some researchers and educational leaders are sold on the longer school day, and I advocate it as well. However, a longer day will not help students if the school is low achieving and filled with pessimism. On the other hand, optimistic schools can produce high achieving students during a traditional six-hour school day.

I strongly advocate single-gender classrooms and schools for Black boys, but if the culture is pessimistic, student performance will be low. But when optimism is combined with single-gender instruction, the sky's the limit for Black boys. Urban Prep in Chicago and Eagle Academy in New York are two excellent examples.

School Leaders

The most important player in the school is the principal. It is very difficult, if not impossible, to change school culture for the better with an ineffective CEO-type of principal. A school's transformation needs a transformational principal. Schools need transformational teachers as well. Just as one or two students can negatively change the culture of the class, just a couple of teachers can negatively affect the culture of the school. It is imperative that the majority speak up. Do not remain silent. Don't let a couple of teachers bring down the culture of your school.

I am always disturbed when the majority remains silent. For example, atheists are only a small percentage of the population, but Christians let them take God, prayer, and the Bible out of schools. German apathy enabled one man, Adolf Hitler, to kill six million Jews. Don't let a small minority change the culture of your school.

Chapter 2: School Culture

Students First

We cannot allow unions to promote the philosophy, "Teachers First". I cringe every time I see this mission statement on bulletin boards. Shouldn't it be "Students First"? "Teachers First" means that high performing teachers who lack seniority are the first to be fired. The low achieving teachers with seniority are protected. Incompetent teachers are allowed to remain in the building because it costs too much to legally remove them. Some superintendents have told me that it takes more than $100,000 to remove an ineffective teacher. In many cases, they are simply transferred from one low achieving school to another.

At the same time, we cannot allow CEO principals to negatively infect the culture of a school and demoralize the teaching staff. CEO principals haven't taught students for the past 20 years, and they only visit classrooms once a year during evaluation time. They subscribe to the cultural deficit model of Black students, and they don't support their teachers. Often they have a personal vendetta against the teachers. Unjustified negative evaluations were one reason why unions sought to protect their teachers.

I recommend, and many school districts have agreed, that evaluations be conducted by both principals and faculty. This one simple change can help transform school culture for the better.

Testing

I am very concerned about the cheating scandal in Atlanta. First, Atlanta is the tip of the iceberg. There were 37 states plus Washington D.C. that have been identified over the past four years. They simply got caught because they were so greedy they exaggerated their progress. Many cities are doing the same thing, but at smaller increments. Second, it shows like on Wall Street and the real estate market, when money is the incentive and people lack integrity they will cheat at any cost. There is no difference between a drug dealer who will sell crack in his community and an educator who will change test answers to receive a bonus. Students were led to believe they had made progress and were promoted when they should have been retained.

Third, this illustrates that placing this much weight on test scores is not only too much pressure on students, it obviously is too much pressure on educators. Fourth, high achieving schools use tests for diagnostic purposes. They test students frequently and use tests to guide their pedagogy and curriculum. They do not allow the test to eliminate art, music, gym, foreign languages and Black history and culture because those issues are not on the state exam. In other countries, they use a variety of testing formats which include; essays, oral presentations and projects. Unfortunately, in America we rely primarily on a multiple choice exam. Many Black students are given 30 minute exams by their teachers while the state gives them a 90 minute exam.

Last, I am very much aware society wants to hold teachers and students accountable. Taxpayers want to see results for their funding. Employers and colleges want to be assured a high school graduate has earned their diploma. The formula cannot be 100% testing. If so, cheating scandals will continue. The formula must include testing, attendance, reduction in remedial reading, special education, suspensions, and dropping out. It should include staff and adminstrator's evaluations. We should also include a component for student and parent input.

We cannot have a culture where either educators or students are cheating. We must have a culture of integrity and honor. Educators could learn from the homeless man who found a backpack with $4000 in cash along with computer equipment. He could have kept the bag but because of his morals and values he turned the bag into his shelter. He was rewarded with over $75,000 in contributions, a job and an apartment!

Chapter 3: Belief Quiz

As you ponder the following questions, keep in mind whether your expectations of Black boys are low or high. Then seek ways to raise your expectations of them.

1. Do you believe that more than 90 percent of Black boys in your school will score equal or above grade level?

2. Do you believe that more than 90 percent of poor children from single-parent homes whose mothers lack a college degree will score equal or above grade level?

3. Is your school fair to Black boys?

4. Are you afraid of Black boys?

5. Do you respect Black boys?

6. Do you believe that some Black boys are bad?

7. Do you understand Black male culture?

8.   What are you doing to bond with Black males?

9.   What is your school doing to make Black males feel important?

10. Do you like Black males?

11. Do Black males like you?

12. Do you see Black males in your school as your sons?

13. Would you send your son to your school?

14. Which teachers in your school would you not want teaching your

son?

Chapter 4: Black Male Culture Quiz

In the chapters that follow, I propose that educators must take the time to learn about Black male culture. As you begin to understand your boys, respect and appreciation will grow. This is the only way that relationships between teachers and Black boys will develop. As relationships improve and boys begin to trust that you genuinely care about them, over time, they will be more receptive to your instruction and classroom management. In turn, the growth of your respect and appreciation for Black male culture may influence your instruction and classroom management.

1. What is your definition of culture?

2. How can people be culturally deprived?

3. What are three Black cultural strengths?

4. What percent of Black males had their fathers in the home in 1920?

    The present? What happened?

5. How do you motivate Black male students to value academics over

    sports and entertainment?

6. What is the greatest problem that Black male students face?

7. How do you feel about the "N" word?

8. How do you feel about saggin'?

9. How do you motivate a Black male to sacrifice short-term wants for long-term gratification?

10. How do you convince Black males that being smart is acting Black?

11. How do you convince Black males that being smart is acting masculine?

12. How do you teach a Black male to avoid a fight and gang membership?

13. What factors turned Malcolm Little into Detroit Red? What factors turned Detroit Red into Malcolm X?

14. What can Black males learn from Frederick Douglass, Paul Robeson, Muhammad Ali, and Imhotep?

15. Name five current Black male athletes, rappers, and scholars.

16. Is your class conducive for picture learners, oral learners, tactile learners, and kinesthetic learners?

Chapter 5: Gender Compliance Quiz

African American males make up 8.5 percent of the student population in America, yet their placement in remedial programs is disproportionately high and their placement in advanced classes is low. Take the following quiz to assess whether your school is in gender compliance with these programs.

1. What percent of your students are Black males?

2. What percent of your AP students are Black males?

3. What percent of your gifted and talented students are Black males?

4. What percent of your honor roll students are Black males?

5. What percent of your A students are Black males?

6. What percent of your students earning F's are Black males?

7. What percent of your retained students are Black males?

8. What percent of your remedial reading students are Black males?

9.   What percent of your special education students are Black males?

10.   What percent of your suspended students are Black males?

11.   What percent of students who drop out are Black males?

12.   What percent of your teachers outside of P.E. are Black males?

Chapter 6: Are Schools Similar to Prisons?

In the Preface, I asked what I consider to be the most important question of this entire book: *Are we sending our boys to college/ entrepreneurship, or are we sending them to prison?* The following questions will help you answer that question for yourself, your school, and school district.

1. What do you know about the schoolhouse-to-jailhouse pipeline?

2. Do some schools resemble prison? Does your school resemble a prison?

3. Is there a similarity between the uniform worn by your students and the uniform worn in prison?

4. Are your school's uniforms inspiring? Do students like wearing the uniform?

5. Does the uniform project what they will wear in corporate America or in prison?

6. Does your school offer differentiated instruction, or is it primarily one pedagogy—a left brain approach?

7. Does your school encourage critical thinking skills? Or does your school simply expect students to complete worksheets?

8. What percent of the school day are students involved in critical thinking? What percent of the school day are they completing worksheets? Reading? Coloring? Listening to your lecture?

9. Is your school a test taking factory? What percent of the school year is spent either taking tests or preparing for tests?

10. How is the décor in your school? Is it inspiring and motivating for students? Or is it drab and sterile, like prison?

11. Is there a difference between the décor in primary grades versus intermediate, upper, and high school grades?

12. Do schools resemble prisons after the primary grades?

13. In prison, the guards often look the other way when there is a fight. In your school, do teachers look the other way?

14. In prisons, the guards have a disdain for the inmates. Bonding does not exist, and there is no relationship. What is the relationship like between your teachers and students?

15. In low achieving schools, large numbers of students are suspended. What about your school? Is your school a suspension factory? What is the relationship between suspensions and prisons?

16. In low achieving schools, a disproportionate number of Black male students are placed in special education. What about your school? Is there a relationship between special education and prison? Is special education a precursor for prison?

17. Are there more Black boys in your schools suspended and placed in special education than in AP, honors, gifted, and talented classes?

18. In prison, cafeterias are dangerous. Fights frequently take place in prison. Do food fights take place in your cafeteria?

19. Restrooms are dangerous in prison. Are your restrooms safe? Clean and sanitary?

Chapter 6: Are Schools Similar to Prisons?

20. In prison, hallways can be dangerous. Are your hallways safe?

21. Are your locker rooms safe?

22. In many schools, there are metal detectors all over the building. Some schools spend more money on metal detectors than on computer labs. Does your school spend more on security than computer and science labs? How do metal detectors affect the psyche of your students and staff?

23. Are parents welcomed in your school? In many cases, prisons and schools treat parents similarly. They are not welcome.

24. In low achieving schools, students can't wait to either drop out or be pushed out. Is the dropout rate a precursor of incarceration?

25. Low achieving schools use outdated curricula. Books are 10 to 40 years old. That is similar to prison. How current are the curriculum materials at your school?

26. Low achieving schools have high principal and teacher turnover rates. In many cases, wardens and guards have more job stability than teachers and principals. What are the turnover rates for the principal and teachers at your school?

27. In many schools, students spend more time in the corner, outside the classroom door, and in the principal's office than they do in the classroom. This resembles solitary confinement in prison. Where do challenging Black males at your school spend most of their time while in school?

28. In many cases, schools are terribly underfunded. Ironically, most prisons receive adequate funding. How interesting that we can find money for prisons, but we can't find money for schools. How interesting; guards without degrees earn more money than some teachers with master's degrees. Is your school well-funded? We could greatly reduce our prison population if provided pre-school education for the 70% of Americans who cannot afford it.

29. Let's compare the wide range of funding that can occur within a state. Some wealthy school districts may receive more than $20,000 per child; every teacher has a master's and above, and every student has a computer. On the other hand, schools in low-income communities, within the same state, receive less than $10,000 per child. Very few teachers have a master's. Twenty-eight percent of the teachers are not certified to teach the subject to which they've been assigned. The only computers in the school are in one room, the computer lab. In contrast, the average inmate receives more than $30,000 in funding. How does this discrepancy in funding make you feel about your school?

30. Is tracking the new form of segregation?

31. Do schools spend more time separating the haves and have nots than educating all students?

32. Is tracking a precursor for prison?

33. Do some principals act like wardens, spending the bulk of their day in their offices and treating their students as if they're criminals?

34. Are we spending more money on security guards than teachers?

35. In many schools, there is a 250- to 500-to-1 ratio of students to counselors. That is similar to prison. How much counseling can go on with ratios like that?

36. Schools are funded based on attendance, not performance. That is similar to prison. Some schools have a dropout rate greater than 50%. Prisons have a recidivism of 85%.

37. Most teachers and prison guards are paid based on seniority, not performance. It is very difficult to remove a low-performing teacher. Does your school have any low-performing teachers and if so, what is being done to remove them?

38. In low achieving schools, the food is terrible. Most inmates feel the same way about their food. How would the students at your school rate the food?

39. In low achieving schools, illiteracy is rampant. Is illiteracy a precursor for prison? More than 80 percent of inmates entered jail illiterate. If we simply taught Black males how to read, we'd have an 80 percent chance of keeping them out of jail.

40. In most schools and prisons, a European culture is promoted. Yet, in prison, more than 50 percent of the inmates are African American. Only 25 percent are European. Which culture does your school mainly promote?

41. Predominately, African American populated schools still teach that Columbus discovered America, Lincoln freed the slaves, and Hippocrates is the father of medicine. Does your school have an Africentric curriculum?

42. The disciplinary policies of many schools are modeled after the zero tolerance policies of police departments. This is identical to the way discipline is handled in prisons. What are the disciplinary policies at your school?

43. In many schools the policy is that students are handcuffed and taken away in police cars. I have read horror stories of primary-grade children being handcuffed and taken away in police cars. Does this happen at your school?

44. In light of the unfortunate tragedy in Newtown, Connecticut, the NRA is recommending armed guards in every school. Some school districts have given teachers the right to carry guns in school. Are schools similar to prison? Is there a school house-to-jailhouse pipeline?

45. Do some schools break the spirits of Black boys?

46. Do prisons break the spirits of Black males?

47. Toilet paper in low achieving schools and prisons is carefully monitored. Does this happen at your school?

Chapter 7: Black Male Culture vs. School Culture

Earlier, I mentioned that there is a cultural disconnect, a mismatch between Black male culture and school culture. In this book, I'm imploring educators to understand Black male culture, to try to make schools more understanding of Black male culture. One of the objectives of this book is to change the paradigm that Black males must come into a world of our design; no, we must go into theirs.

Following are some of the ways Black male culture is disconnected from school culture.

Black Male Culture	School Culture
Fighting	Tell an authority
Play	Study
Video games	Reading
Incomplete homework	Completed homework
Aggressive	Passive
We	I
Cooperation	Competion
Short-term gratification	Long-term gratification
Rap	Reading
Music	Math
Sports	Science
Street IQ	School IQ
Crack	Ritalin
Don't cry	Cry
Don't ask for help	Ask for help
Don't need a tutor	Accept a tutor
Not pleasing the teacher	Pleasing the teacher
No snitching	Snitching
Thug	Sissy
Honor roll without study	Honor roll with study
High self-esteem/low school-esteem	High self-esteem/high school-esteem

The only way for us to enter the world of Black males is to first respect their world, and understanding will surely follow. For example, parents and the streets teach Black males that if someone hits you, hit him back. Yet, the school rule is to tell someone in authority. That is a cultural disconnect, a cultural mismatch.

I'm not suggesting that we should let students hit one another, but we need to have a discussion with students about these two approaches as they relate to fighting. In addition, we need to hear when Black males say that they did tell the teacher, but nothing happened. The teacher did not resolve the conflict. Now the conflict has escalated and the student has to walk home. He needs protection. Or the student has been suspended. This is more unsupervised time away from school. This cultural disconnect is a recipe for disaster.

Later in the chapter on the peer group, we will discuss the cultural dichotomy between "we" and "I", cooperation and competition. This is very important in understanding the culture of Black males.

The last thing a Black boy wants is to be isolated from his peer group. There's a very important reason why Black boys don't want to be in advanced classes: they don't want to be separated from their friends. Schools where Black males have performed well in AP, honors, gifted, and talented classes have understood how increasing the number of Black males in those classes increases their success overall.

In the next chapter, we will look at classroom management.

Chapter 8: Classroom Management

I believe there are two types of parents and teachers as it relates to discipline. We have authoritative and permissive parents and teachers. Permissive teachers have major classroom management problems. They want the students to like them and let them determine the rules. Authoritative teachers want and demand their students to respect them. They determine the rules and the rules are clear, visible and enforced. They encourage student input and they listen to them, but the final decision is made by the teacher. Some teachers have a higher suspension rate than others because of poor classroom management skills. We could reduce the suspension rate and the number of boys placed in special education if teachers improved their classroom management skills.

I was once asked to speak at a particular school where they had major disciplinary problems. As usual, when schools bring me in, they want me to fix the bad Black students. So I politely asked the principal, "Before I fix the bad Black students, may I observe your most challenging group in three different periods?"

In periods one and two, the children were unruly, undisciplined, not on task, and they did not respect authority. When I showed the videotape I made of those two periods, the teachers just loved it because their position was reinforced. They felt vindicated. There was nothing wrong with the teaching staff; it was those bad Black children.

Then I showed them my videotaped recording of the third period class which was taught by a White female teacher in her 60s. This teacher embraced good teaching. Her students were not simply reading textbooks, completing worksheets, coloring, listening to her lecture or watching a video. They were debating, analyzing, discussing, writing, and discovering. They were using critical thinking to solve problems. The rules were clear in the class. There was movement in the classroom. The students were on task. There was a spirit of optimism in the classroom, and the students appeared to really love learning. It was as if they had gone to another planet and learned a concept called "selective discipline"—they respected this older White female teacher, but not the African American female and younger White male teacher of the first two periods.

Black students are not as affected by the race or gender of the teacher as they are by whether the teacher genuinely cares for them. What I love about students is that they lack tact and diplomacy and are quick to call a spade a spade. You cannot fool Black males. I am reminded of a story told by professor Pedro Noguera. A teacher was having a problem with classroom management and was encouraged to observe a master teacher. During the class, a student called the teacher a B. The teacher calmly went over to the student and said, "would you call your mother a B? Everytime you see me think of your mother!" You don't learn that in college. You learn that from knowing the culture of your students. The teacher played the dozens with the student.

I asked the staff, "Do you want me to talk about the bad students in periods one and two, or do you want me to talk about period three and what good teaching looks like?"

African American students were never the problem. Those teachers had to accept that classroom management skills of the other teachers were lacking. Some teachers think classroom management is hollering and telling students to sit down and shut up, while they sit in their seat. I am asking teachers if they could go one week without hollering and saying shut up and sit down. Teachers can reduce disciplinary problems if they rely less on textbooks, worksheets, videos, coloring and lectures. Students cause more problems when they are bored and disengaged. Classroom management should not be based on the cemetery model: Line them in rows and keep them quiet.

Know Your Students

In this chapter, we will look at how teachers can improve their classroom management skills, especially relative to Black boys. The first step is to understand your students. You can't manage them if you don't know them. Let's look at the various types of Black male students. Read on to learn how to recognize them and help them reach their full potential.

Class Clown. Many teachers do not know how to handle the class clown. In co-ed classrooms, there's a much greater chance that a class clown is going to be male. There are many reasons for this. Class clowns have large egos and are usually underperforming academically. They are ashamed of their academic deficiencies, so they act out to cover up their insecurities. They want attention, and they want to be removed from class. When a Master Teacher is cognizant of why the class clown is acting out, the last thing he/she will do is remove him from class.

The class clown thinks he's funny, so call his bluff. Give him an opportunity in the last five minutes of the school day to perform. Let's see how funny is the class clown. If he's not funny, he won't be a class clown much longer. If he is funny, then you might be a catalyst for his career.

Most importantly, explain to the class clown that the reason why you are allowing him his five minutes of fame is because of his academic deficiency. Tell him that you're willing to arrive early, give up part of your lunch, and stay late to work with him on his deficiency. It is great to watch a Master Teacher convert a class clown to a scholar. If we want to improve school culture for Black males, the teaching staff must learn how to transform class clowns into scholars.

Chapter 8: Classroom Management

Because you know the class clown has a large ego and desires attention, give him as much attention as possible, but be careful with his ego. *Do not embarrass him.* The male ego is very large and fragile. Boys are more sensitive than we think. When a teacher does not like them, they can sense it, and it hurts. If boys know you don't like them, they won't care about learning for you or from you. What's more, your disdain will negatively impact their academic performance and will also contribute to disciplinary problems. Males have a tendency to keep their deepest feelings locked up inside. You may never know how they feel. But if you can try and like your Black male students, you will begin to observe an improvement in academics and behavior.

The class clown is also very good at playing the dozens, signifying, cracking, and ranking. In White culture, words are taken literally. In Black culture, words are figures of speech. Many Black boys have been suspended, placed in the corner, and removed from class because they were playing the dozens, a verbal word game around the most prized person in Black culture: Mother. Ironically, the game is designed to avoid a fight. White teachers, who take words literally, think the boys are about to fight. But the boys created this game to avoid a fight. They want to find out who's the best, who's the strongest, and who can handle the harshest words about Mother. After playing the dozens, the boys will continue being the best of friends, but if their White teachers don't understand the dozens, they'll send the boys to the principal's office. There is a disconnect between Black and White culture.

We can ill afford to make this critical mistake. We must understand the motivation behind the dozens. Now please do not misquote me or misunderstand me. I'm in no way condoning the dozens. We should not allow students to talk about each other's mothers in class. But I do think we need to appreciate the culture of our students as well as the fact that it takes a lot of verbal skill to be a good dozens player. For example, you need to have an expansive vocabulary, and you need to know how to make words rhyme. You must feel comfortable speaking and being dramatic in public. You need to be able to think quickly on your feet.

Encourage your best dozens players to join the spelling bee team, try out for the drama club, and compete in the debate team. Your best dozens player should be the MC at all school programs. They should be involved in spoken word exercises. Let's empower the dozens player because he has skills that can be used to earn an A in language arts. He can use those skills to become a rapper, a lawyer, a politician, a civil rights activist, and a broadcaster. We must connect school culture to Black male culture.

The Sleeper. I cringe every time I see an African American male student who has been allowed to sleep in class. Parents should know that some teachers would rather have their sons sleep in class rather than cause them grief. As a result, students are disengaged from the academic process for two-thirds of the school day. Master Teachers and Coaches who believe in Rule 110 do not allow students to sleep in class. I believe only Custodians, Referral Agents, and Instructors allow students to sleep. Master Teachers and Coaches think too much of themselves and value their students too much to allow them to sleep in class.

When a student falls asleep in class, walk over to him, call his name, or touch his shoulder. Do whatever is necessary to wake him up and let him know that sleeping is not allowed in class. There could be some special circumstances causing this behavior, so make sure you find out what's going on at home.

Many times the problem is not that they're sleepy. They're simply making a statement. They are intentionally showing disrespect to the teacher. The student is saying, "I don't like what you're teaching. I don't respect what you're teaching, and I'm going to make a statement to you by going to sleep in your class." Not only is he refusing to listen to you, he's going to show the rest of the class that he's not listening to you. One to three teachers can change the culture of the school, and one to three clowns or sleepers can change the culture of a class. It's a disease that can spread. So the first time you see any student sleeping in your class, you have to catch it immediately.

So wake him up. Unfortunately, in most classrooms students are sitting the entire day. It is tragic, especially with the high rate of child obesity. Children are sitting from 9:00 to 3:00 with maybe five or 10 minutes of recess, P.E. once a week, and a 20-minute lunch and menu that may put them back to sleep!

When you wake up your sleeper, make sure you have something for him to do. Have him pass out papers, pencils, and pens, or send him to the principal's office with a note. Do whatever is necessary to get these students on task. In the special education chapter, we will discuss how to allow more movement in the classroom. One of the best ways to prevent sleeping in class is to provide more tactile and kinesthetic lesson plans.

The Quiet Student. I believe that nearly one-third of Black male students simply fall through the cracks. They seldom cause any problems. They don't behave like class clowns. They don't sleep in class. They're simply quiet. They're in the middle academically. They may not cause any disciplinary problems, but they don't thrive either. They stay mediocre. I wonder how many great scholars we have lost because they were allowed to fall through the cracks.

Every classroom teacher reading this book should make a list of the students who are in the middle and are not reaching their full potential. There's something missing in them and in your pedagogy. Later, when we discuss leadership, we will delve further into what could be done with these quiet students. These are the quiet, passive students in the middle, and while you may be thankful that they don't cause problems, the truth is they deserve your attention just as much as your clowns and sleepers.

Love Your Students

There's a tremendous distinction between "All children *can* learn" and "All children *will* learn because of what we do." The statement, "All children can learn" is too passive. It suggests that the potential is there, but it may not happen this year or in your classroom. The statement "All children *will* learn because of what we do" reflects your high expectations of students. It shows your personal sense of responsibility for the children in your care.

Educators, repeat the following affirmation daily:

> "Under my watch, during this school year, my children will learn regardless of race, income, gender, or educational background of the parent. I am the teacher the students have been waiting for. I refuse to let you fail."

Do your children learn for you? Let's say a student misbehaves and you say, "You really disappointed me." If you do not share a bond, the student could care less about disappointing you. When bonding takes place, then they will learn for you. Ideally, they will learn for you and for themselves. Your respect and genuine caring for their welfare can be very motivational for students. It will get to the point where they won't want to disappoint you or themselves. This seemingly small beginning will lay a strong foundation for learning and enhanced self-esteem.

If we're going to change school culture for Black males, we must understand that relationships are even more significant than resources. You could have a school that allocates more than $20,000 per child, a computer for every student, every teacher has a masters and beyond, but if the teacher has not bonded with the students, then education is not going to be maximized. Academic achievement will be greatly reduced.

Teachers, you cannot teach a child that you do not like. Many teachers do not like or respect Black boys. Why, then, are you teaching Black boys? My request is that you do not teach children that you do not like. You're hurting these children, and that's not fair to them. Your ability to be successful, your efficacy, is greatly reduced when you don't like your students.

You cannot teach a child, a Black male, whose culture you do not appreciate. If you believe that Black males are culturally deprived, you have compromised your effectiveness. You have to believe that Black males have cultural strengths. You need to know those strengths. You need to use those strengths in all of your subjects.

You cannot teach a child, a Black male, when you're afraid of him. Many teachers are afraid of Black boys. In low achieving schools filled with pessimism, ineffective teachers are placed in the primary grades, and the only advantage they have over their students is their size. When students become unruly, they use their size to discipline them. Stronger teachers are placed in the upper grades because they have much better classroom management skills. This approach is not helping anyone, certainly not the students or the teachers for that matter.

If we're going to improve school culture, our best teachers should be placed in the primary grades. It is unfair to upper-grade teachers to have to correct inadequacies that formed in the earlier grades. In most states, high stakes testing begins in third grade. Many principals are unaware of the problem that has been festering since kindergarten. While it is never too late, we don't need to find out Willie is 2 years behind in reading when he takes the third grade state exam. We're burning out too many upper-grade teachers with problems that should have been circumvented in the primary grades.

Principals should have their best teachers teach kindergarten. Short of removal, the least effective teacher should be placed in eighth grade. Hopefully, if a student has had excellent teaching in the primary grades, he should have such a big lead that if, God forbid, he has an ineffective teacher in eighth grade, it won't devastate him. He'll still be performing at grade level and probably above.

If we can have the better teachers in the primary grades, teaching and instilling discipline, motivation, a love for learning, and critical thinking skills, then there's a very good chance that whomever students will experience in the upper grades, the resources, talents, and behaviors they developed early on will be an established part of their mind-set and behavior.

If there is a shortage of effective teachers at your school, then starting in the primary grades, consider looping students with strong teachers. Two consecutive years of an ineffective teacher could destroy a child for life; two consecutive years with a Master Teacher or Coach will produce a scholar.

Remember: 20-25 students, three/ four years at a time. I'm appealing to principals, administrators, and educators to give Master Teachers 20-25 Black boys from kindergarten through second grade and then from third through fifth, assign another Master Teacher the same 20-25 students. Give them another master teacher sixth through eighth grade or if your school requires departmentalization give them the same subject teacher for the next 3 years. The same concept applies to high school. They will have the same master teacher for 4 years in each subject.

Chapter 8: Classroom Management

Now consider these words:
- Like
- Respect
- Culture
- Fear

I'm reminded of Alisha Kiner, the principal of Booker T. Washington High School in Memphis, Tennessee. Her school was an underperforming school, and the graduation rate was less than 50 percent. Since the school was in recovery, she had the right to pick and choose her staff. Her major requirement of incoming staff was, "If you want to teach in this school, you must love the students." I like the audacity, strength, and fortitude of this principal. She was determined to raise the bar beyond just liking and respecting her children. She said, "You must *love* them." If we are serious about improving school culture for Black boys, we need to love Black boys.

A curriculum of love encompasses more than a hug. It includes high expectations and not accepting inferior work. It requires listening to them and offering constructive criticism and encouragement. You are willing to tutor them before or after school and during lunch. You are in touch with the parent and visit the home. You think about them often like your biological children. You are concerned about their well being and their future aspirations. You invite them to weekend activities. You enjoy being in their presence and express interest in staying in touch in subsequent years. In light of the above, do you love your students?

We have to master the concept of bonding with Black male students. One of my most frequent workshop requests is on bonding. How do you bond with African American male students? Every time I give this workshop, I really feel that the staff wants me to give them a pill or some quick solution that they can use to bond with the students. Naïvely, over my almost 40-year career, I have tried every way possible to give them the pill in 30 to 45 minutes. The reality is that you *cannot* bond with African American male students if you don't like them, if you don't respect them, if you don't understand their culture, and you are not a friend to them. Now with that in mind, let me now attempt to give you a "pill" on how to bond with African American male students.

1. In addition to calling them by their name, call them "son." Refer to them as "sir" "mister" and "scholar."

2. *Have students discuss their career goals*. Once they tell you their career aspirations, for the rest of the school year, refer to them based on their career. Always connect their career goal to the progress of

their work. Remind Willie that he won't be an engineer or doctor with a 30 or 40 math or science score.

3. *Male students are the stars of the classroom*. Without these students, you would not have a job. Therefore, I recommend that you ask them to bring in a photo of themselves to place on the walls of your classroom. They need to know they are the stars of the classroom.

4. *Motivation*. This will take a little research, but identify famous African American males who have achieved success in various careers— engineering, medicine, law, etc.—and post their pictures next to students who have similar interests. Throughout the year, not only will the students get a chance to look at themselves, they'll get the chance to look at an adult Black male who has achieved in their career. Later in the book, we will look at the tremendous impact that sports and rap have had on Black males. When you ask students their career goals, do not allow them to give a career in sports or entertainment.

5. *Inspiration*. Bring in a photo of yourself, but not a current photo. Bring in a photo of yourself as a child in the same grade you're now teaching. If you're a fourth-grade teacher, bring in a photo of when you were in fourth grade, or as close as possible. Children love to see that their teacher was not always an adult and that he/she was once their age. It's even better if you can, from time to time, share some of the challenges you experienced in that particular grade.

6. *Engagement*. Teachers often tell me they don't have time to bond with their students or make the curriculum more relevant (because we live in an era of high-stakes testing, etc.). However, research and my own observations have shown that students are only engaged one-third of the classroom time. Children are doing things other than being on task during the school day. The time students spend in the corner, outside the classroom door, and in the principal's office could

be greatly reduced if we mastered these bonding principles. You can pay now or pay later. So if we are willing to allocate time during the day to bond with students, it may reduce some of the time we're losing in other areas.

7. *Smile at your students every day.* All students, especially African American males, need someone to smile at them. They need words of encouragement and someone to listen to them.

8. *Give students a hug.* What the angriest students in class causing the most disciplinary problems with a scowl on their faces really need is a hug. I'm aware that we can't touch students even though that goes in one ear and out the other with Master Teachers. They will put a hand on a shoulder, give a high five, shake a hand, rub their back— they find ways to let students know they care.

9. *There's a science to classroom seating.* If a teacher does not like a student, more times than not that student will sit as far away from the teacher as possible. In addition, he/she will seldom come close to the student. Where do your Black males sit in your class? Where do you spend the bulk of your day in your classroom? Don't think that Black males are not cognizant of where they sit and where you are throughout the school day. Oral and visual learners should sit in the front.

10. *Relevant curriculum.* If you want to effectively bond with your students, you have to make the curriculum relevant. Students want to ask, "Why do we have to learn this?" If you've bonded with the students, they will be comfortable asking that question, and you will be comfortable answering. You should know your curriculum well enough that you can connect it, regardless of the subject, to students' neighborhoods, sports, entertainment, or whatever you feel resonates with Black male students. Another way to make curriculum relevant

is to have the students identify an African American male whose success matches the student's interests or career choice and have the student tell this man's story verbally or in writing.

11. *Align pedagogy with learning styles.* There should be congruence between pedagogy and students' learning styles. If you want to effectively bond with your students, you won't teach the way you want to teach. You will teach the way your children learn. Therefore, during the first week or two of the school year, ascertain what percent of your students are right brain learners and what percent are left brain learners. Don't give left brain lesson plans to right brain learners. Determine what percent of your students are visual print learners, picture learners, oral learners, tactile learners, and kinesthetic learners. Later, in the chapter on special education, we will examine learning styles in more detail. If you want to effectively bond with your students, provide lesson plans that match their learning styles.

12. *Rule 555.* Five percent of students cause 95 percent of classroom problems. Those problems occur in the first five minutes and the last five minutes of the class period. If you want to observe Master Teachers at their best, observe them during the first five and last five minutes of the class period when students tend to act up. Students know when teachers are not prepared, and they act up. When students complete their work early and they have nothing to do during the last five minutes, they act up. We must give those who finish earlier additional work. To improve academic outcomes, teachers must be at their best in the first and last five minutes of the class period, and they must be on the lookout for the five percent of students that are causing 95 percent of the problems.

13. *Rule 110.* All children *can* learn is not good enough; I challenge you to raise the bar to all children *will* learn. Before integration and Brown

vs. Topeka, teachers, both Black and White, taught from Rule 110. In other words, 100 percent wasn't good enough. Students had to go above and beyond to 110 percent. Teachers used to demand the best of Black students, regardless of their socioeconomic situation. Later, in the chapter on racism, we will discuss this in more detail. We cannot lower our expectations for Black male students because of their race and gender. We must raise our expectations and expect the best of them. Never again accept mediocre or substandard work from your students. Demand the best of your boys. If you want to improve your school culture, see your students as capable of delivering 110 percent.

14. *Time on task.* One of the best ways to convince students that you care about them, that you want to bond with them, that they are important to you, is to let them know you're available. If they need help, be available. Come to school 30 minutes early. Be willing to give up your lunch hour to tutor students. Be willing to stay 30 minutes after school. This will ensure greater time on task.

15. *Parental involvement.* Are you willing to exchange phone numbers with your parents? Are you willing to call them? Parents want me to remind you to please call them every once in a while with good news. Most parents say the only time they hear from teachers is with bad news. If you want to bond with your students and parents, then periodically call with some good news. Email and text some good news. Post a positive note on their Facebook page, or Tweet a note. Find ways to communicate good news to your parents. In addition, if you really want to improve your bonding experience, walk students home and personally introduce yourself to parents. I commend school districts that have made home visits mandatory, but even if yours doesn't require this, voluntarily visit your students' homes.

16. *Weekend field trips.* Periodically take one or two students or the entire class on an outing so that you can be involved with each other outside of the classroom. One of the best ways to determine if you've bonded with your students is if they come back to visit you. I can almost guarantee that if you make home visits, call parents, and take students on outings, they will never forget you. You will be their teacher for life. They will learn *for* you, not just from you.

17. *Home training.* If your students come to your class lacking home training and respect for authority, then teach them the principles and rules of home training, and do it with love and respect. I realize how difficult it is to teach a child who lacks home training and respect for authority. Some teachers spend more time disciplining children and they deal more with attitudinal issues than classroom issues. If you decide it's not your job to teach home training, then be prepared to spend more time disciplining than teaching.

18. *Master Teachers have clear rules.* Rules are discussed at the beginning of the year. The rules are posted on the board, so students see them every day, and there's no doubt about their meaning. Also, Master Teachers are fair. They are willing to hear both sides of the story in order to fairly assess what happened and who did what. Then they fairly enforce the rules. Children become confused when you enforce the rules with one student but not with another, when you have one rule on Monday and another on Wednesday, when you make statements like, "Don't do what I do. Do as I say." We must be clear, consistent, and fair.

Good Teaching

What does good teaching look like? What are good principles of classroom management? How do we change the culture to maximize academic achievement for all students, and especially African American males?

Chapter 8: Classroom Management

Often when I visit a classroom, I see one of five things taking place. Students are either reading a textbook, completing a worksheet, listening to a boring lecture, watching a boring video or coloring. Ironically, I see upper-grade students still involved in coloring. Some teachers think they are becoming more high-tech by having students watch videos. I have no problem with videos, especially for visual picture learners, but I am concerned about teachers thinking they can simply push the play button and 40 minutes later, push the stop button. Good teaching transcends textbooks, worksheets, lecturing, coloring books, and videos.

I love observing classrooms where students are engaged in academic conversation, where they are analyzing, debating, and writing about the issues. They are learning based on discovery. Critical thinking is taking place. If we want to improve school culture for African American male students, we must release our dependency on textbooks, worksheets, lecturing, coloring books, and videos. Infuse your pedagogy with more conversation, writing, debating, discovering, analyzing, and critical thinking.

Differentiated Instruction

A popular topic in education today is differentiated instruction. For example, there may be 30+ students in one fourth-grade class, but in reality, students are performing at three or more different levels within the same class—for example, 10 at third grade, 10 at fourth grade, and 10 at fifth grade level. While ideal for the 10 at the fourth-grade level, it hurts the 10 at the fifth-grade level and frustrates the 10 at the third-grade level. Differentiated instruction is a tremendous challenge for teachers who must design at least 3 different lesson plans for students who not only are performing at different grade levels, but have different learning styles (print, picture, oral, tactile, and kinesthetic).

Unfortunately, many teachers of these classrooms tend to teach to the middle. Later, when we discuss peer culture, we will look at how cooperative learning can be used with great efficacy. Consider putting students into learning groups and mixing up the levels within each group. They would learn from each other. There are many ways we can offer differentiated instruction.

Before moving on to the next chapter, I'd like to leave you with the following poem written by a Black male student:

Will You?

Will you greet me with a smile and have encouraging words to say?
Will you appreciate my learning style and coach me along the way?
Will you provide images of role models who look like me?
Will you expect me to become all that I can be?
Will you notice my hand when it goes into the air?
Will you call on me so that I know that you care?
Will you have a relevant curriculum when teaching the class?
Will you establish a relationship and allow enough time on task?
Will you inspire me to dream until my dreams come true?
Will you insist that nothing less than excellence will do?
Will you value me and see past my race, gender, poverty and my parents?
Will you believe that I will make a contribution to this great nation?

In the next chapter, we will look at what we can do to improve the language arts skills of Black boys. Black boys love to communicate through the dozens and rap, so why is it so difficult to teach Black boys how to read and write?

Chapter 9: Language Arts Culture

The term "language arts" encompasses not just reading but also writing. If you think we have a challenge teaching Black boys how to read, we have an even greater challenge teaching them how to write.

Literacy is the civil rights issue of the 21st century. How is it that the richest country in the world, a country that has the ability to send rockets to Mars, finds it so difficult to teach Black boys how to read and write effectively? If we do not teach Black boys how to read, we almost guarantee them a prison sentence.

Only 12 percent of African American males are proficient in reading by eighth grade.[7] That means that by eighth grade, 88 percent of African American males are behind in reading. Illiteracy is the precursor for retention, special education, dropping out, and incarceration. So many times when school districts bring me in, they want me to address how they can reduce their retention, special education, suspension, and dropout rates. Social services agencies want to know how they can reduce the incarceration rate.

Well, the answer is simple. Teach Black boys how to read. More than 70 percent of Black boys in special education are not there because of ADD, ADHD, LD, or ED. They're there because they are behind in reading. And Ritalin will not solve illiteracy. We could improve reading scores if we simply gave all Black children a vision test. Unfortunately, almost 25% are in need of glasses. They need glasses not Ritalin! We have found that the lowest 10% of students primarily suffer from lack of sleep not Ritalin. Can you imagine if we simply work with the parent to address this issue we could improve academic achievement?

If you thought the 12 percent figure was staggering, consider this statistic: if a child is behind in reading at the end of first grade, he has only a 20 percent chance of graduating at grade level in reading.[8] That is staggering. A school district will spend $10,000 or more per child per year but only 20 percent of students between the second and 12th grades will be proficient in reading! What happened? What did not happen? Are our expectations of our boys so low that we have given up on them?

What strategies and solutions could be implemented at your school that would improve literacy for African American males? And that question brings me to the great debate between phonics and whole language.

I'm reminded of the book Rudolph Flesch wrote in 1955, *Why Johnny Can't Read*. Nearly 30 years later he wrote the sequel, *Why Johnny Still Can't Read* (1981). I encourage you to read both books. The author documents that in the 1950s, America moved from phonics to whole language instruction, and there's been a steady decline in reading scores ever since.

This is not just a Black male problem. Educators tell me they include phonics in their repertoire of reading strategies, yet more than 50 million Americans are illiterate. What percent of your reading curriculum is phonics-based?

A good test of your system is if your students can pronounce my name. It is difficult to pronounce my name using the word or sight approach to reading, but if you understand phonics, it is easy to pronounce my name. Research shows that if a child has mastered phonics by third grade, there is no word they cannot pronounce.[9]

I believe the problem of African American male literacy transcends the great debate between phonics and whole language. Unfortunately, Black males resist reading. Until educators understand the cultural significance of this resistance, this problem will persist.

I'm reminded of the doll study conducted 1939-1940, by the husband and wife team of African American psychologists, Kenneth and Mamie Clark. Black children were given a Black doll and a White doll, and then they were asked to choose. This research fueled the Brown vs. Topeka civil rights case of 1954. If you place a basketball, football, baseball, television, iPod, video game, or book in front of a Black male adolescent, which one will he not choose? We must do what we can to increase the odds that if given a choice, Black boys will choose reading. We must change this culture of Black males that says being smart is acting White and feminine and that literacy is for girls, not for boys.

Many factors are driving this problem. For example, educators refuse to consider gender and maturation differences in learning. Research shows that girls mature faster than boys. There is almost a three-year difference between kindergarten and 12th grade. Unfortunately, boys are expected to learn how to read at the same pace as girls. Not all boys are ready to read in preschool, kindergarten, first, or second grade. There is nothing wrong with the boy. He should not be placed in special education and given Ritalin because he did not learn or have a desire to read at the same time as girls. Later in the book, we will dissect this in more detail. Suffice to say here that if we want to change the culture for Black males, then we must allow for maturation differences between boys and girls. No longer should we expect boys to learn how to read at the same time and pace as girls.

This does not negate the fact that some boys mature at the same rate as girls and that some parents have made reading a top priority for their sons at a very early age. But we need to accept that a number of boys have not learned to read at the same time as girls and were not blessed with parents who made reading paramount. As a result, they are behind girls as early as first grade.

Who selects the books in your school? Have you ever asked Black boys what types of books they would like to read? What titles and authors they might enjoy? Ask them what they would like to read, and their answers might surprise and delight you.

Most books are selected by female teachers for female students in most schools. The specific interests of boys are rarely considered when purchasing books for schools and classroom libraries. And teachers wonder why Black boys aren't reading.

It is imperative that educators provide materials that most boys like to read. The operative word here is "most." Most Black boys, not all, do not like reading romance novels or books on relationships. They do not like reading long books. They do not like reading fiction unless it's science fiction. Most boys like reading books about sports, rap, cars, technology, animals, and biographies about people that look like them.

African American Images has designed a collection of books called *Best Books for Boys*. We have asked boys what types of books they like to read. We've also researched genres and authors that resonate with Black boys. We have found that boys like reading for information, not necessarily enjoyment. They like reading books and articles that provide information that can be used in practical ways.

Teachers tell me that Black boys lack reading comprehension skills. Yet if you give a boy the manual for his DVD player, iPod, iPhone, iPad, or Xbox he has no problem reading the manual and putting the apparatus together. Research shows that many adults cannot read or comprehend the manual for their DVD player and then record a show. So I'm not convinced that Black boys lack reading comprehension skills. However, if they are reading something that does not interest them, their comprehension is affected.

Visit your school library, or look at the collection of books in your classroom. Now imagine yourself as a nine- to 13-year-old male. Which books would Black boys read?

Let your boys read through some publishers' catalogues, and let them choose the books they want to read. We need to put boys in the center of the curriculum. We need to empower them and make them feel important. We could solve the literacy problem if we simply provided a selection of books that was geared toward Black male culture.

I once overheard a Black male student tell a teacher, "I hate this book. I want a book that talks about me. I want to see me in this story." I could not have said it any better.

As you are selecting books for your school and classroom library, I strongly recommend that you purchase the following:

- *You Don't Even Know Me: Stories and Poems about Boys* by Sharon Flake
- *Handbook for Boys: A Novel* by Walter Dean Myers
- *Narrative of the Life of Frederick Douglass*
- *The Autobiography of Malcolm X*
- *The Contender* by Robert Lipsyte
- *Hip Hop Street Curriculum: Keeping It Real* by Dr. Jawanza Kunjufu

I also encourage you to read Alfred Tatum's book, *Teaching Reading to Black Adolescent Males: Closing the Achievement Gap.* He has done an excellent job of helping educators understand how literacy is a lifeline for African American males.

Have your boys read Frederick Douglass' autobiography. During slavery, Whites would do everything possible to make sure that Africans were not taught how to read. Douglass realized how important literacy was for his freedom, so he would sneak out at night, and by moonlight or candlelight, teach himself to read. Often he was caught and beaten almost to death. Every time they beat him, it inspired him to read more. What secret knowledge, what power was in a book that Whites didn't want him to know?

Now juxtapose Douglass' experience against the fact that today boys seem allergic to books. They don't want to be seen by their friends taking a book home to read for homework or pleasure. Something has happened to our boys between 1850 and the 21st century. If we're going to correct this problem, we need to connect those dots between Frederick Douglass and our boys in the 21st century.

Find posters that show adult Black males reading and put them all over your walls and bulletin boards. Invite adult Black males to read to your boys. We need to make reading important, cool, and masculine. We need to make it pervasive in the lives of our students.

Have your boys read together in small groups. We want to make reading fun and cool and acceptable to boys, so offer a prize, not to an individual, but the group that reads the most books in a week, month, or school year. The prize should be significant, such as a trip to Disney World, a basketball game, or an amusement park.

Writing

If you think literacy is a problem with boys, the problem is compounded with their writing skills. This problem transcends race. Research shows that the writing gap is greater by gender than race or income. White males score much lower than White females and even females of other races. Females from low-income families have higher writing scores than many middle-class White males. This shows how acute is the writing problem. What is of even greater concern is that now, one-third of the score on the SAT and ACT is based on proficiency in writing.[10]

Chapter 9: Language Arts Culture

I'm reminded of the books *Boy Writers: Reclaiming Their Voices,* where they say, "My hand hurts!"[11] Many boys, because of gender differences, are behind girls in fine motor skills. As a result, boys may be slow in getting up to speed with their writing skills. They cannot hold a pen for long periods of time without their fingers hurting. We need to give them more time rather than punishing them for not writing at the same rate of time or speed as girls. Yet, on the other hand, they don't seem to have a problem using their fine motor skills to play video games. There seems to be a disconnect or missing ingredient that could improve writing skills among boys.

Many teachers do not encourage boys to write about their interests. Some boys are into violence and aggression, which is frowned on by female teachers. Let's use language arts to empower Black males. Asthma and lead poisoning are major problems in many Black neighborhoods. Require your students to investigate the matter. Why is it so prevalent in some communities? Have them write letters to politicians. Is a longer paper better than a shorter one? Are boys penalized because their papers are shorter than females'? Should we grade boys' writing qualitatively or quantitatively?

So it all comes down to interest. If Black boys have the opportunity to read books they enjoy and write about issues that are significant to them, then reading and writing proficiency will increase. Have your boys write journal entries daily. Give a significant prize to the group (not an individual) that have the best entries. Identify what constitutes a "good" entry by focusing on the quality of an entry—such as its originality, development, and topic, etc. They should write about what's going on in their neighborhoods, the good things and the problems. Have them write about their sports team, gym shoes, and favorite rappers. The topics may not be interesting to you, but they are to boys. Let us pick our battles. If the goal is to increase reading and writing proficiency, then let them read and write about topics that interest them.

Time on Task

To improve reading and writing skills, we must address the issue of time on task. One of the major reasons for the success of the KIPP Academy, Urban Prep, and 3,000 plus high achieving schools is that most have a longer school day. Black boys spend more time playing basketball and video games and listening to rap than they do reading and writing. Schools must allocate more time during the school day for phonics instruction, writing, and reading culturally relevant books. What good is an extended school day if you're still teaching whole language and making Black boys read Eurocentric, feminine books? First, allocate more time in the school day for reading and language arts. Many schools provide an additional hour or two after school for reading. Second, assign books that will be interesting to Black boys.

How about connecting reading to basketball? In order to play in the basketball league and compete in the championship game, members of the cooperative learning groups must be in the top reading group. Let's say you have 12 cooperating learning groups of male students in your classroom or school. The top four or so groups who read the most books and write the best articles would be eligible to play in the basketball championship. There is no need for this to be oppositional. We don't need to separate sports from academics. One can complement the other. This approach will convince boys that it's cool to read and write well.

Unfortunately, I don't feel a sense of urgency or passion to help Black boys. I commend schools that understand how critical it is to improve the 12 percent proficiency by eighth grade, but those schools are far and few in between. We need more principals serving as instructional leaders and more teachers working with one another to improve the culture and learning outcomes for Black boys.

I recommend mastery of content. The only acceptable grades are A, B, and C. If you do not master the content you must repeat the class. The grade D should not be acceptable and males are earning 70% of these grades. It is a tragedy to observe a 16 year-old male freshman with less than 6th grade reading skills. We must abolish social promotion. Many principals have told me they are mandated by their board to pass students. They have a quota on how many students they can retain. We cannot change school culture with this mindset. Schools must take some ownership in retention.

We must place our best teachers in the primary grades to insure boys will master reading. Many schools rely heavily on the state exam to assess their students. What happens to Black boys when they are socially promoted kindergarten thru second grade and then the state exam which is first given in third grade illustrates they are behind in reading? Who will teach them how to read in fourth grade? This could have been circumvented with primary grade master teachers, less reliance on the state exam and abolishing social promotion.

The alternative is to allow for a gender maturation difference, allow boys to read when they are ready, read books that interest them and offer more single gender classrooms. We must teach to their learning style and provide books they want to read. The reading mantra is we teach how to read in primary grades and you read to learn in upper grades. The dilemma is if you have not learned how to read in primary why are schools sending students to higher grades where you read to learn if they can't read?

If we don't solve this reading crisis, we will see an increasing number of Black boys in our next chapter on special education.

Chapter 10: Special Education Culture

By now you know that African American boys are disproportionately placed into special education programs— and seldom are they prepared to mainstream back into regular classes. If a student needs special attention, then there should be a beginning, middle, and an end to his involvement in the program. No child should enter special education without an exit strategy in place. For example, one measurable goal would be that the student will be reading at grade level by the end of the school year.

If we're going to improve school culture for Black males, we must honestly address the following questions:

- Why are boys of all races placed in special education more than girls?
- Why is there a 2:1 ratio of White boys to White girls in special education?
- Why is there a 4:1 ratio of Black boys to Black girls in special education?
- Is there something wrong with boys?
- Do educators want boys to act like girls?
- Is female behavior the norm, the standard?
- Is *different* synonymous with *deficient*? Because boys are different than girls, does that mean that boys are more deficient than girls?
- Have we designed a female classroom for male students?
- When was special education legislation created? (The answer is 1975.)
- What did schools do with challenging male students before 1975?
- Was special education legislation designed for female teachers to rid themselves of challenging males?
- Was special education designed for White female teachers to rid themselves of challenging Black males?
- Why do we call it "special"?
- Do boys go there for X number of years and return to the mainstream classroom at grade level?
- Do you know what percent of special education students are mainstreamed at grade level?
- Did you know that many Black boys in special education are fearful of returning to the regular classroom because they know they are not on grade level?
- What percent of special education students graduate on grade level with a diploma and not a certificate?

Boys want to be successful at whatever they do, and they know by fourth grade if school is going to be effective for them. They definitely know that special education will not make them competitive when, and if, they return to the regular classroom.

Why do teachers send more boys to special education than girls? Why are Black boys sent more often than White boys? Earlier, I mentioned the teacher I call the Referral Agent. Research shows that 20 percent of the teachers make 80 percent of the referrals to special education. Yet in most schools, the Referral Agent doesn't receive an honest evaluation, punishment, or training, and the behavior continues. How can a referral agent receive an excellent evaluation? What percent of teacher referrals are approved? How are boys treated by a referral agent if their referral was not accepted?

It is true that teachers are dealing with overcrowded classrooms that include a few challenging students—class clowns, dozens players, sleepers, and thugs. If they can get rid of these students, that makes the classroom much more manageable. Unfortunately, the Master Teacher or Coach who seldom refers male students to special education receives no salary increase or award. There are no incentives to keep students out of special education. Yet Master Teachers and Coaches work with their students under challenging conditions and do extremely well.

I would understand if Master Teachers and Coaches became discouraged. What makes it worse, in some schools, the Referral Agents are dictating the culture, and they are encouraging other teachers to mimic their approach and refer more students, more males, to special education. Yet teachers with a mission and a love for their students march on, despite the less than ideal circumstances.

The IEP Meeting

The Individual Education Program (IEP) meeting is one of the most important meetings in a student's life. Many Black parents (usually a single mother) have suffered through such a meeting. It is very intimidating for the low-income, single mother who probably lacks a college degree to defend herself and her son in this meeting. Let us dissect what occurs in an IEP meeting.

The purpose of the IEP meeting is to review the recommendation of the Referral Agent. Typically in attendance will be the principal, psychologist, social worker, special education coordinator, classroom teacher, and parent. Without a doubt, the IEP meeting is very intimidating to parents. The meeting is scheduled for Wednesday at noon, which means it is designed for the professionals, not the parent. The parent has to miss work to attend the meeting because the professionals are unwilling to come back to school after hours for the parent's convenience. That's a cultural decision.

72

Chapter 10: Special Education Culture

The meeting may have been scheduled for 12:00, but the professionals arrive 30 minutes early to discuss their positions in order to present a unified front to the parent. They meet intentionally without the parent present. There is a culturally driven code of silence and agreement among the professionals. This also occurs in police departments.

The professionals don't always agree. There could be at least one or two professionals who feel that before placing the child in special education, they should provide more right brain lesson plans for the child. They advocate understanding and then teaching to students' learning styles. They suggest providing more lesson plans for picture, oral, tactile, and kinesthetic learners. They want to meet the need of the student instead of the staff. It's a cultural decision, when the professionals decide it's better to go along and get along with their peers.

To improve school culture for African American males, we need to overhaul the approach of the Referral Agent. I'm impressed with many schools that have created pre-referral intervention teams of Master Teachers. Before a child is sent to special education, these teachers will observe the Referral Agent in the classroom and make suggestions for improvement. Not only is this a sensible approach, it is compassionate. It is student-centric. In my book *Keeping Black Boys Out of Special Education*, I share 86 mainstreaming strategies that pre-referral intervention teams are using to help Referral Agent teachers, and more importantly, keep Black boys in the mainstream classroom. We have seen a major reduction in special education placement when a strong pre-referral intervention team is in place. That's the kind of cultural change we need.

School cultures must be transformed so that when a Referral Agent sends a child to special education, a process automatically kicks in to intervene in the behaviors of teacher and student. Policy and culture should make it difficult for these teachers to remove students from their classrooms. The new and improved school culture should provide training and mentorship to Referral Agents. IEP meetings should be more conducive for parents than staff. Professionals should not feel obligated to align themselves with one another. The child must come first, not the staff. That's the kind of cultural change we need for Black boys.

Transforming the Female Classroom

Have we designed a female classroom for male students? You can answer that question by asking yourself this: How would an ideal male classroom look? Ask your Black male students to write about how an ideal male classroom would look?

Can you imagine, we could reduce special education placements if we simply offered P.E. on a daily basis. Some schools are now being designed and constructed without playgrounds. With more than one-third of our children either overweight or obese, why is P.E. only offered once a week for 20 to 40 minutes at many schools? If we want to change school culture for Black males, P.E. should be offered on a daily basis for a minimum of 45 to 50 minutes.

We could reduce special education placements, if we simply gave boys recess. Some schools have actually taken recess out of the schedule. Other schools take away recess to punish boys for misbehaving—when they should be giving *more* time for running around and playing. Behavior can improve with recess. How many adults can sit rigidly still in a chair from 9:00 am to 3:00 pm with the only break being a 20-minute lunch? That's the way we've scheduled the school day for active, energetic, dynamic, high octane boys. Just doesn't make sense. No wonder they're climbing the walls in your classroom.

How would an ideal male classroom look? Well, you would not have students being required to sit in their chairs all the time. We need to pick and choose our battles. I see nothing wrong with a Black male student standing behind his table not a desk, as long as he's on task. Boys like to stretch out and a table is more conducive than a desk. There's nothing wrong with a student standing behind his table with a ball in one hand and a pencil or pen or book in the other. There's nothing wrong with a boy shooting a ball into a basket whenever he answers a question correctly. What's wrong with him giving another student a high five when he gets an answer right? We must welcome Black male culture into classrooms and schools.

There's nothing wrong with students moving from one learning center to another. They are on task, but they are moving from the writing center to the oral center to the picture center to the fine arts center to the tactile center to the kinesthetic center. In stagnant, dead classrooms, students sit quietly and still for long periods of time, by themselves, coloring pictures of Columbus supposedly discovering America. In dynamic classrooms where students are engaged with the learning process and culturally-relevant lesson plans, there's movement, there's analysis and debate, and they are on task.

We could reduce special education placements if we redefined teaching as more than students reading a textbook, completing a worksheet, coloring, listening to a lecture or watching a video. We could reduce special education placement if we allowed more discussion, more writing, more analyzing, more debating, more discovering, and more use of critical thinking skills. Some teachers may think they are meeting the needs of their auditory learners by lecturing. A lecture would be fine if it was less than 15 minutes. Oral instructions not lectures are better for auditory learners. Putting concepts to rhyme, jingles and music are excellent. Providing music in the background is ideal. Lectures that are short, vibrant, louder, with changing pitch are great. Oral learners love stories, small group discussions, debates, and oral reports and exams. They love to hear their voice not yours.

We could reduce special education placements if we allowed Black boys to ask, "Why do we have to learn this? How does this concept help me stay safe in my neighborhood? How does this concept empower me?" We could reduce special education placements with cooperative learning groups.

How do we explain two public schools (not magnet or charter) in the same neighborhood, with the same demographics, and yet School A has less than five percent of students in special education and School B has 25 percent? Can this be explained by race? Income? Gender? Parental education? The answer is no. Both schools have the same demographics. The answer can be found in school culture and the leadership styles of both principals.

The principal of School A is committed to keeping Black boys in the mainstream classroom. Referral Agents are challenged. The pedagogy of Master Teachers and Coaches is aligned to their boys' learning styles. They offer differentiated instruction and excel in bonding with their students. Unfortunately, in School B, the ineffective teacher in Room 201 never gets a chance to observe the Master Teacher in Room 203. Moreover, School B never visits School A to see what they are doing right.

Now let's go a level higher than the principal of both schools. If the superintendent does not provide instructional leadership for the entire school district, if he/she is simply a CEO of the district, then the problem will continue systemically. The culture of the entire district needs to change.

Is your school's special education program in gender compliance? What percent of your students are African American male? What percent of your special education students are African American male? If you have a disproportionate number of Black male students in special education, then you are out of compliance. What is your school going to do to become compliant? Have you provided your staff with a workshop on gender learning styles?

Let's recap the major gender differences and how schools should adjust.

Gender Differences

Male Characteristic	School Adjustment
Shortest attention span	Shorten the lesson plan and/or gear lessons toward male interests.
Less developed in fine	Lower penmanship, handwriting, writing and cursive expectations.
Greater energy level	Allow more movement and exercise through the day.
Less hearing ability	Speak louder, have boys sit closer to the front, and understand why boys are louder.
Slower maturation	Allow for the differences, especially in reading, and eitheravoid comparing boys to girls or create single-gender groups within the class.
Not as neat	Alter expectations, assist them and provide more organizing time and tools.
Less cooperative	Understand that most boys are not teacher pleasers and desire greater male influence. Consider inviting male role models to speak to your class.
Influenced more boy peer group	Never embarrass him in front of his peer group. Consider implementing cooperative learning and peer tutoring.
More aggressive	Understand the showdown, the dozens, and the need for boys to resolve conflict. Provide nonviolent, physical opportunities to achieve this, e.g., Native American band wrestling.

In closing, let's be honest. Do some schools place Black boys in special education for financial reasons? We must change that culture. Are Black boys being placed in special education because some White female suffer from "I fear Black Boys Syndrome?" We must change that culture.

Writing Assignment

Have your male students write the names of their friends who are in special education, and then have them interview these students about how they feel about being in special education. Have them write about how their friends perceive special education.

We will now move to the next chapter which describes the suspension culture in too many schools.

Chapter 11: Suspension Culture

What percent of your students are African American male? What percent of the students suspended in your school are African American male? Is your school in racial-gender compliance regarding suspensions? Did you know that:

- Nationwide, one of six African American males is suspended.
- One of 14 Hispanic males is suspended.
- One of 20 White males is suspended.[12]

In some school districts, almost 50 percent of Black male students are suspended. Some schools are literally suspension factories. The culture says suspend first, ask questions later. Have you ever wondered:

Why are so many Black males suspended?
Why are males suspended more than females?
Why are Black males suspended more than Hispanic males?
Why are Black males suspended more than White males?
Are we afraid of Black males?
Can you teach a child who you fear?
Does racism have anything to do with so many Black males being suspended?

Racism is a subject that we don't want to talk about, but we will discuss it in depth in a later chapter. I marvel when my White peers and I present the same information, but because they're White, it is received better. I encourage you to read the work of Russell Skiba, *The Color of Discipline*, and the work of Daniel Losen. These two brilliant White scholars document the pervasiveness of racism in the suspension culture of many schools populated by African American males.

For a White male to be suspended, one of three things has to be present: a gun, a knife, and bloodshed. For a Black male to be suspended, there doesn't have to be a gun, a knife, or bloodshed. He can be suspended because the teacher does not like the way he looks at her. She does not like the way he walks. She does not like his tone. She does not like what he says. She does not like his eye contact. She does not like the fact that he walks away from her. She does not like his swagger. Can you imagine, a Black male is suspended because of his swagger!

Fairness is critical when it comes to changing school culture. Children of all races and both genders, but especially Black males, experience problems with favoritism and the lack of fairness when it comes to being disciplined. For example, three of the most popular reasons for suspension are possession of a cell phone, attire, and tardiness. Skiba and Losen document that both White and Black males commit the same infractions, but White males tend to be given multiple warnings while Black males receive suspensions. [13]

We can offer all the books, workshops, seminars, and conferences to educators, but until we call it what it is, until we call a spade a spade and racism as racism, until we acknowledge that educators have been racist in their treatment of African American male students, unfair discipline will persist. As you might expect, the largest school districts with the highest percentage of Black male suspensions, some as high as 50 percent, are in predominately Black communities. However, the race of the teaching staff may not reflect the race of the student body and community at large, and that might be a factor in the high suspension rates of these schools. Just because a school is predominately Black doesn't mean the teaching staff is predominately Black. In fact, it is probably mostly White.

I have spent the last four decades in these schools, and I've seen the racial demographics of teachers change. Since 1954, there's been a 66 percent decline in African American teachers. [14] In some schools, there's not one Black male in the building. If a Black male is there, I will wager that he is the janitor first, a security guard second, a P.E. teacher third, an administrator fourth, and a classroom teacher last.

In some schools I've visited, the student body is 75 percent African American, but the teaching staff is 75 to 90 percent White. Often the principal will be African American, but that doesn't mean he/she has been able to change the culture. In these schools, you'll see from one out of six Black boys suspended to *one out of two*; these rates are unacceptable.

Skiba and Losen document how schools in the same neighborhood, with the same demographics, can show startlingly different suspension rates. School A suspends one out of 20 African American males; School B suspends one out of six and School C one out of two. Same community, same demographics. How do we explain this? Everyone loves looking at the social issues—the race of the parent and student, the gender of the student, the income of the student, the involvement of the parent, the educational background of the parent—but how do we explain this huge suspension gap between schools?

The answer is school culture. School A has a strong principal who has taken the position that suspension is the last option in the school. Every effort will be made to keep the boy in the classroom, on task, and engaged in the academic process. Other schools suspend first, discuss later. In some schools, the principal lacks the backbone and leadership to demand more of the staff. In these low achieving schools that have become suspension factories, the inmates are running the asylum.

If we are serious about African American males, we cannot allow these suspension factories to persist. There should be an outcry, an urgency, a passion to find solutions to the high suspension rates of some of these schools.

We need to study success and not failure. What are Urban Prep, Eagle Academy, and 3,000 plus successful schools doing to change the culture for Black boys? What is it that some schools are doing to reduce their suspension rate? There is nothing wrong with Black boys! We must change the culture.

Classroom Management

One of the most effective ways to reduce the number of Black male suspensions is good classroom management. Remember the White female teacher I mentioned earlier? Her children were on task and engaged in learning. Significantly, in the earlier two periods, one teacher was African American the other was a White male. It's not the race, gender, or even age of teachers that makes the difference with African American students. It's teachers' effective classroom management skills, high expectations, understanding of learning styles, and ability to bond with students.

Clearly racism exists, but it is not the only factor. Before the murders in Newtown, Connecticut, many schools were cutting counselors, social workers, psychologists, and teacher aids while adding more security guards and metal detectors. In the aftermath of Newtown, now we have the NRA and other authorities recommending the arming of principals and teachers. Are schools becoming more and more like prisons? We must not allow fear to compromise our good sense. Arming principals and teachers and increasing security guards and metal detectors will not reduce the Black male suspension rate. These approaches will only add to the culture of fear that is being created, with the NRA's help, at many schools. It is very difficult to teach and learn in a school that is fearful.

Instead, let us investigate and implement classroom management strategies that have been effective with Black boys. Let us bond with students, not fear them. Let us understand and teach to their learning styles. If we can just do these things, we will have a culture of optimism in our schools, which is conducive to teacher efficacy and engaged learning.

Unfortunately, in suspension factories, there is fear, disdain, and disrespect between staff and students. In these factories, the policy of zero tolerance is pervasive. On the other hand, schools with lower suspension rates implement policies of grace, mercy, and forgiveness. They like their boys. They're not afraid of their boys. They welcome the culture of Black males into the school and classroom.

I believe there's a hatred of Black boys in suspension factories. Ironically, many of these schools have an African American principal, 10-20 percent African American staff, and "liberal" White teachers who would never act "that way" (i.e., be racist). Yet unfortunately, they have allowed their schools to become suspension factories. A negative, pessimistic culture permeates throughout these schools, and again I say, the only way to reduce the suspension rate is to change the culture.

There is a small light at the end of this very long tunnel, however. Suspension policies are slowly but surely changing across the country. Many districts are beginning to see how their unfair, racist practices have enabled Referral Agents to suspend Black boys more than any other group of students. New policies include a moratorium on Black boys being suspended unless they are in possession of a knife or gun.

This moratorium on Black boys being suspended needs to be enforced nationwide. In fact, we could avoid and reduce suspensions if we simply allowed Black boys to cool off. Before you suspend another boy, give him a drink of water first. Allow him five minutes to relax and calm down. Walk with him for at least five minutes or shoot some hoops. Try and assess if words were spoken in true anger or if this was just a game of the dozens between two boys. If it's the dozens, the boys may have been trying to avoid a fight. If you're quick to judge behaviors that are culturally unique, you may misconstrue the situation and suspend them both. Many times what the teacher thought was a fight was actually two males determining where they were in the pecking order. You see this in sports all the time. Two athletes get in each other's face selling wolf tickets. They are trying to sense if there's fear and how much heart the other person has. Next thing you know, they're the best of friends.

Speaking of pecking order, did you know that there's a pecking order in your classroom? Many teachers naïvely think that they are in charge of their classroom. The reality is that one to three students are running the class, and they are influencing the other students. You need to know the pecking order of your class. You must understand the dynamics of the Alpha male. There is a battle in your class on who will be the Alpha male. Who are the most influential students? Who's the number one male student in class? Unfortunately, the most academically gifted male is probably the least respected, and the struggling male is the most respected or feared.

Next, you must empower the most influential students in your class. They need to become your assistant teachers. In fact, let them sometimes teach the class. One single mother told me that her son was chosen to teach a few classes in his high school, and this definitely boosted his self-esteem. It also gave him a lot of respect for what teachers do every day. Students need to be positive role models for one another. Use them in a way that's beneficial for you rather than detrimental to students. Convert your Alpha males to class captains and watch your disciplinary problems decline.

Next, we must reconsider the *way* suspensions are implemented. When Black boys feel they are not liked, respected, understood, and nurtured by their teachers, they devise schemes to get suspended. Out-of-school suspensions are like vacations for boys. Why would you give a truant a 10 day suspension? Many will act out just to get thrown out. They *want* to be suspended. Clearly, as a punitive measure, out-of-school suspensions do not change behavior.

When it is truly necessary to enforce strong discipline, let's give them an in-school suspension. Not only will this help working parents feel secure in the knowledge that their children are being supervised in school, students will feel the pain a little more when they have to continue to attend school, do homework, read books, write papers, do calisthenics, and read more books. There should be *more* schoolwork designed for them, not less, as would occur in a traditional suspension.

I call my favorite in-school suspension programs the "Dr. King Classroom" and the "Malcolm X Classroom." In the Dr. King Classroom, we teach Black boys how to resolve conflict through nonviolence. In the Malcolm X Classroom, we teach leadership skills, showing students how Malcolm Little was converted to Detroit Red and how Detroit Red was converted to Malcolm X.

I'm also in favor of peer mediation and restorative justice. More schools should use the peer group to address the needs of students and to mete out discipline fairly. One of the most effective components of implementing fairness, not zero tolerance, would be where students, under adult supervision, implement mediation and restorative justice programs for their schools. I encourage you to study the great research that has been conducted around peer mediation and restorative justice.

I commend educators in the state of Maryland who realized that the suspension rate was contributing to the dropout rate. It is very difficult to matriculate to the next grade if you've been suspended for 10, 20, 30 days out of the school year. In the next chapter on dropout culture, we will look at this in more detail. But there is a correlation between a high suspension rate and dropping out.

Would you suspend your son for all the infractions that you have suspended your Black male students for?

Would you suspend your son because of the way he looked at you?

Would you suspend your son for the way he walked? The way he talked? His tone of voice? His eye contact? His swagger?

Would you suspend your son because he was in possession of a cell phone? Or because of his attire? Or because he was late for school?

I'm simply asking teachers to treat Black boys the way they would treat their sons.

Can you imagine teachers, principals, and schools calling the police to discipline their sons?

Can you imagine a six-year-old boy being handcuffed, walked through the corridor in front of his peers, placed in a squad car, placed in a holding cell, and his parents having to pick him up from the police station?

Would you want your son to be handcuffed and paraded through the corridor? Would you want your son to be placed into a police squad car and taken to the police station? Is there such tension, fear and disdain between educators and Black boys that it has come to this?

Before 1954 and Brown vs. Topeka, when we had one-room school shacks, this did not take place. We had more teachers who believed in Rule 110. We had teachers like Marva Collins, who took the position, "You will learn, and I can teach." We did not have this. Something has happened in the culture of these schools. What was once a nurturing one-room school has now become a suspension factory, and police have now become our assistants.

What was once a nurturing one-room school has now become a schoolhouse-to-jailhouse pipeline.

Writing Assignment

Have your boys write a paper that addresses the following questions:

Have you been suspended? Was it fair?

Is your school fair?

What teachers are unfair in your school?

Write all the names of the people you know who have been suspended in your school.

Do you prefer in-school or out-of-school suspension? Why?

Chapter 12: Dropout Culture

Is your school a dropout factory?

Is your school in gender compliance with regard to dropping out?

What percent of your students are African American male?

What percent of your dropouts are African American male?

How do you define a dropout? Some schools define their dropout rate based on the percentage of seniors who do not graduate. Obviously, those schools will have a much lower dropout rate than schools that calculate the number of freshmen that actually graduated four years later.

Many factors can determine graduation and dropout rates. In some schools, the student turnover rate is nearly 50 percent each year. Some schools and school districts have a difficult time tracking the migration patterns of students who must move frequently with their families. For example, a student who enters a school as a sophomore may leave in his junior year and graduate (or not) from another school. How do you determine the dropout rate for your school or school district in this scenario?

Some advocates feel that the dropout rate should not be calculated on a four-year schedule, but more like five or six years. This is similar to college, where less than 33 percent of freshmen graduate four years later. Others feel that the dropout rate is exaggerated because large numbers of students, specifically African American males, earn their GED by age 25. There's been an interesting debate between the Schott Foundation and the producers of the excellent documentary, *Hoodwinked*. The Schott Foundation believes that the dropout rate is approximately 48 percent while the producers of *Hoodwinked* feel the rate is nearly 25 percent. Listed below is the national dropout rate as measured by the Schott Foundation.[15]

State Graduation Data

Throughout this report, graduation rates below the national averages, and gaps above the national averages are shown in red. Numbers are rounded to the nearest whole number.

Table 1
BLACK/LATINO/WHITE, NON-LATINO MALE GRADUATION RATES BY STATE

| | 2009-10 Cohort | | | | |
| | Graduation Rates | | | GAP | |
STATE	Black	Latino	White, non-Latino	Black/ White	Latino/ White
Alabama	53%	58%	69%	15%	11%
Alaska	71%	93%	70%	-1%	-23%
Arizona	84%	68%	82%	-2%	14%
Arkansas	59%	69%	73%	14%	3%
California	56%	64%	83%	26%	19%
Colorado	56%	46%	75%	19%	29%
Connecticut	59%	56%	85%	26%	29%
Delaware	47%	52%	68%	22%	16%
Dist. of Columbia	38%	46%	88%	50%	42%
Florida	47%	58%	62%	15%	4%
Georgia	49%	52%	65%	17%	13%
Hawaii	60%	60%	39%	-21%	-21%
Idaho	73%	73%	79%	6%	6%
Illinois	47%	59%	81%	34%	22%
Indiana	49%	70%	80%	31%	11%
Iowa	41%	*	90%	49%	—
Kansas	54%	62%	80%	27%	18%
Kentucky	58%	62%	69%	11%	7%
Louisiana	49%	63%	63%	14%	0%
Maine	97%	*	86%	-11%	—
Maryland	57%	62%	81%	24%	19%
Massachusetts	60%	53%	83%	23%	30%
Michigan	54%	58%	80%	25%	22%
Minnesota	65%	59%	89%	24%	30%
Mississippi	51%	50%	62%	11%	12%
Missouri	56%	72%	81%	25%	10%

Chapter 12: Dropout Culture

The Urgency of Now

| STATE | 2009-10 Cohort | | | | |
| | Graduation Rates | | | GAP | |
	Black	Latino	White, non-Latino	Black/White	Latino/White
Montana	63%	71%	82%	18%	10%
Nebraska	44%	80%	86%	43%	7%
Nevada	52%	48%	61%	8%	13%
New Hampshire	60%	83%	80%	20%	-2%
New Jersey	63%	66%	90%	27%	24%
New Mexico	49%	57%	62%	13%	5%
New York	37%	37%	78%	42%	41%
North Carolina	58%	50%	71%	13%	21%
North Dakota	*	*	*	—	—
Ohio	45%	54%	80%	35%	26%
Oklahoma	64%	64%	76%	12%	12%
Oregon	72%	74%	77%	5%	3%
Pennsylvania	57%	59%	85%	28%	26%
Rhode Island	64%	57%	75%	11%	18%
South Carolina	46%	45%	62%	16%	18%
South Dakota	65%	62%	81%	16%	19%
Tennessee	62%	63%	76%	13%	13%
Texas	53%	55%	75%	22%	21%
Utah	76%	62%	84%	7%	21%
Vermont	82%	87%	81%	-2%	-6%
Virginia	54%	62%	77%	23%	16%
Washington	55%	56%	74%	19%	17%
West Virginia	62%	71%	69%	7%	-1%
Wisconsin	55%	68%	92%	38%	25%
Wyoming	59%	74%	78%	19%	4%
USA	52%	58%	78%	26%	20%

Indicates inadequate data for analysis.

The producers of *Hoodwinked* found the rate to be 25%r if you allow for mobility that occurs with some students between their freshman and senior years, if the dropout rate is based on a span of five or six years, and if you factor in the number of African American males who earn their GED by age 25.

Bottom line, whether you believe the dropout rate is 50 percent or 25 percent or somewhere in between, it is simply too high. The dropout rate did not begin in 12th grade or ninth grade. Boys know early whether school is going to be effective for them and help them navigate their lives.

The dropout rate can start as early as kindergarten, when teachers begin tracking students into various reading and math groups. The reality is that the boy could have dropped out in kindergarten when he was placed in the lowest reading and math group and subject to the low expectations of his teachers. He dropped out when the teacher did not provide lesson plans congruent with his learning style. He could have dropped out when he was expected to learn how to read at the same pace as girls, but because he did not do that, he was placed in remedial reading—without phonics and without a selection of books that he enjoyed.

He could have dropped out when he was retained. Over the years there has been much discussion on retaining students. Research shows that when you retain a child for one year, there's a 50 percent chance he will drop out. If you retain a child for two years, there's a 90 percent chance he will drop out.[16] Some educators and researchers suggest that social promotion, where students are promoted from one grade to another for social and psychological reasons, not academic proficiency, will reduce the dropout rate. They argue that retention negatively impacts self-esteem, so it's better to let students matriculate to the next grade, regardless of whether they can keep up with the curriculum and their peers.

Some schools retain students and place them with the same teacher, same lesson plans, same pedagogy, same low expectations, all the while expecting a different outcome. That's insanity. Reducing the dropout rate means that we must radically and dramatically change our approach to educating students who are on the fast track to failure and dropping out.

As much as I've been an advocate of building the self-esteem of Black boys, I'm not in favor of promoting a child to the next grade if he has not been able to master the previous grade. There is nothing more frustrating for a student entering the ninth grade with fourth grade reading and math scores. How can you possibly teach algebra and biology to students with fourth-grade skills?

I'm in favor of retaining students. An excellent study that came out of New York looked at two groups of students. One group was retained, but given better teachers, greater time on task, and a more challenging curriculum. The other group was promoted to fifth grade. They evaluated the students in eighth grade. The students of the group who had been retained were now back on grade level. [17]

These students can also benefit from right brain lesson plans, cooperative learning, and single-gender classrooms.

It's not fair to put the burden of the dropout rate solely on the shoulders of high school staff. High schools should not have to assume 100 percent of this burden, especially when the problem began in elementary school, even as early as kindergarten.

K–8 schools must share the dropout burden. To all schools I ask: Where is the urgency? Where is the passion? Where is the zeal? Where is the concern? The dropout rate for African American males is unacceptable.

Can young Black males be successful today without a high school diploma? In this challenging economic climate, high school dropouts are not competitive in the job market.

Earlier, we mentioned that only 12 percent of African American males are proficient in reading by eighth grade. If a child is behind in reading by the end of first grade, there's only a 20 percent chance he will graduate on grade level in reading. That's where the dropout rate begins. It is difficult to graduate if you are deficient in reading. Illiteracy is the precursor for the dropout rate. We must channel all of our resources and expertise to teach Black boys how to read. If we don't teach Black boys how to read, if we don't produce students on grade level, then we undermine their ability to graduate from high school.

Looping

I advocate looping with Master Teachers and Coaches. Two consecutive years of ineffective teachers can destroy a child for life, and so schools should never loop students with Custodians, Referral Agents, and Instructors.

From the fourth grade on, one of the factors that contribute to the dropout rate is departmentalization. Not all children do well with four to six teachers per day. If we want to change the school culture for African American males, we need to reconsider departmentalization.

I understand that teachers can't teach all subjects, but I do believe that even at the high school level, we can reduce the number of teachers that our boys are exposed. A student does not need four different language arts teachers in high school, nor do they need four different language arts teachers between fifth and eighth grade. They don't need four different math teachers fifth through eighth or ninth through 12th. They don't need four different social studies teachers fifth through eighth and ninth through

12th. They don't need four different science teachers fifth through eighth and ninth through 12th. They surely don't need four different P.E. teachers fifth through eighth and ninth through 12th.

Bill Gates was on to something when he focused on making schools smaller and more intimate. The saddest story is when African American male students drop out of school and no one misses them. No one knows they're gone. One of the reasons is the number of counselors in inner city schools. It's not unusual to have 4,000 students serviced by only four counselors, which means only one counselor per 1,000 students. Schools that are surrounded by gangs, drugs and homicides need more counselors and support staff. This investment is much cheaper than prison. Very little counseling is going on in these schools. It is easy for struggling Black males to get lost in the system. These schools are dropout factories, and we need to make them more intimate. Relationships are more important than resources. Schools must become student- and male-friendly.

Reduce the number of teachers our boys are exposed to, and increase the number of counselors. monitor departmentalization, and allow African American males to loop with Master Teachers or Coaches from kindergarten through high school.

High School

I mentioned that high schools should not have to shoulder the entire burden for the dropout rate. Despite the odds against success, some high schools in Baltimore, Houston, Bridgeport and other parts of the country are doing a fantastic job. They have allocated tremendous resources to monitor students. In Bridgeport, the superintendent personally along with his staff visited the homes of students who had dropped out. Half the students returned back to school because they realized someone cared.

Unfortunately, many schools literally have to become babysitters. One of the precursors for dropping out is chronic absenteeism. Schools can determine which students are at risk of dropping out from their absentee rates. When some students are absent almost 25 percent of the school year, is it really fair to expect the school to do what the parent should be doing, and that's to make sure that her child is in attendance on a daily basis?

I could have easily written another book about changing parent culture for Black males. The first responsibility of a parent as it relates to education is to make sure that her child is in attendance on a daily basis. Unfortunately, some parents are not doing that. I commend schools for allocating the resources, especially in these economic times, to visit homes, patrol the streets, call the parents, and do whatever they must to ensure the student is in school.

Chapter 12: Dropout Culture

Some parents say, "He left home. I thought he was going to school, but unfortunately he never made it." So schools not only have to visit homes, they must patrol the streets.

Just like the White House has a War Room or Situation Room, some schools have similar rooms where they monitor students. They need to know exactly where they are at all times. Some students did make it into the school, but they did not stay in the school. So they must monitor their movements throughout the school day to make sure they stay inside the building.

One of the major issues facing Black males is the tension between the school and the street. The streets are pulling on African American males. Later, we're going to look at peer pressure, drugs, gangs, sports, rappers, and prison. We're going to look at the impact the streets have on African American males. For too long, schools have had a very distant relationship to the streets. If we want to change school culture for African American males, educators must have a better understanding of the tremendous influence of the streets.

Boys want to be successful. If they find that school is not going to help them, they will look for alternatives. Unfortunately, some boys are convinced that the streets—selling drugs and engaging in other criminal activities—offer a greater chance of success.

When a 16-year-old with fourth-grade reading skills can sell crack cocaine and earn more than $1,000 per week, you don't have to be an engineer to assess which one offers him the most hope.

An excellent documentary, "Dropout Nation" that aired on *Frontline* in 2012, looked at the dropout crisis in America. One of the young African American males featured was chronically absent from school. Why? He had an abusive, alcoholic father, a crack-using mother, and he had to babysit six children. So his gang became his family. He was unsupervised from 3:00 pm until he decided to come home. He was a teenage father at 15, and he was four years behind academically. This is how life is for some African American males in some inner city communities.

How do we successfully change school culture? How do we reduce the dropout rate for a 15-year-old who is chronically absent, living with an abusive father, a drug-using mother, having to take care of six siblings, a member of a gang, unsupervised in the afternoon and evening, and a teenage father who is four years behind academically?

I commend schools and school districts that have created a sense of urgency and passion to address these social ills. I encourage you to listen to the documentary on Harper High School in Chicago. The school is in one of the poorest neighborhoods. The community is gang and drug infested and there have been numerous murders of students. Almost every student knows someone who has been murdered. The government does what is correct and provides them with extra social workers, psychologists, deans, administrators and security officers. They realize this is more cost effective than sending them to prison at a cost over $30,000 per year with a recidivism of 85%. Unfortunately, due to the same politics seen between schools, unions and school boards, the state and federal government withdraws the monies almost every four years. Why do we cancel funding for schools that have successfully changed the culture of their school? Are we as a society, serious about the well being of our students or is it true –Teachers First-School Board First-Politcians First? Prison First?

I encourage you to read the excellent book by Kevin Hall, *Mentor or Die.* As mentioned, many schools have a dearth of African American males in the building. Kevin Hall documents that mentoring can reduce the dropout rate up to 50 percent for boys. I encourage all males to join Susan Taylor and the National CARES Mentoring program she founded. Everyone needs to be mentored, but especially African American males. Only 28 percent of them have fathers in the home. Less than one percent of elementary school teachers and less than 10 percent of high school teachers are African American male. Too many boys are not being nurtured or given direction by adults who look like them.

If we want to change school culture for African American males, if we want to reduce the dropout rate, consider implementing a mentoring program in your school. Remember our mantra: 20-25 boys, three/four years at a time. Provide mentors for each boy. This would be an excellent way of not only improving school culture for African American males, but reducing the dropout rate.

Writing Assignment
Have your Black male students write about the following questions:
What is the future of a high school dropout?
Write the names of all your friends who dropped out of school and describe what they are doing.
Do you think you will drop out?
What keeps you in school?
What about school encourages you to drop out?
What makes the streets attractive?

In the next chapter, we will look at the impact of the peer group on African American males.

Chapter 13: Peer Group Culture

Of all the chapters in this book, this may be the most important. There is no influence that has a greater impact on African American males than their peer group. If we're going to successfully change school culture, we must address the peer group.

Listed below is a historical snapshot of influences on male behavior:
- 1960 – home, school, church
- Present – peer group, music, television/video games

The peer group is all-important to Black boys, but teachers do not factor this into their pedagogy or lesson plans. You do not embarrass a Black boy in front of his peer group. There is nothing he values more than his peer group. You do not send a boy to the board to do a problem, if you aren't absolutely sure he will do well because of how much he values his peer group. You do not ask a boy to read aloud in front of his peer group, if you aren't absolutely sure he is going to do well.

There is a direct relationship between age and peer pressure. As a boy becomes older, peer pressure increases. Peer pressure is a major contributor to the fourth-grade syndrome because by fourth grade, the African American peer group tends to discourage academic achievement. Educators and parents may be doing an excellent job, but a boy's friends have more influence than they do.

From the intermediate grades on, we must understand the impact that peer pressure has on African American males. There's also a correlation between self-esteem and school-esteem. Often, principals will invite me in to speak to their male students, and they want me to help them build up the students' self-esteem. I really want to ask the principal, "Have you observed your boys on the playground, in the neighborhood, in the corridors, in the cafeteria, anywhere outside of the classroom? I don't see low self-esteem among African American males. I see low *school*-esteem." Dr. Jason W. Osborne agrees.

"A study of 15,037 teenagers points out an alarming trend among black teenage boys that helps explain their poor academic performance. Dr. Osborne found that unlike other teens, the self-esteem of black adolescent boys becomes less and less linked to academic accomplishment as they move through their high school years. By the time they reach 12th grade, there is no statistical relationship between the academic accomplishment and self-esteem. He found that failure to identify positively with academic achievement was a major predictor of absenteeism, truancy, dropout, and delinquency among students. If a student's identification with academics is diminished, he will feel neither personally rewarded by good school performance nor punished by poor performance. This is what's happening to black teen-age boys. Black adolescent boys suffer more than any other group because the stereotypical beliefs about them are very, very negative. These kids are often perceived very harshly by teachers, principals, and others in authority. They are frequently considered menacing and less able to perform academically than other teenagers. In short, they are expected to fail."[18]

Dr. Osborne's research is significant. Many boys have disidentified with school. They no longer use school as a barometer of their success or failure. They simply do not care. African American males will not be academically successful if they have disidentified with school. If they don't care whether they are literate, if they don't care about their GPA, if they don't care whether they are in AP, honors, gifted, talented, regular, remedial, special education, or retained classes, helping them raise their test scores becomes next to impossible.

We must find ways to help Black boys reconnect with school. We must help them see a correlation between school-esteem and self-esteem. Many boys are withdrawing from school as early as kindergarten and have decided to pursue other paths. They are defining for themselves what makes them important, significant, and positive. When students have disidentified with school, they definitely do not care about whether or not they disappoint the teacher.

I often ask my audiences to visit a kindergarten class. There you will observe boys sitting in the front of the class, eager, curious, on task, and learning. Then I ask them to visit a ninth-grade class. There you will see the exact opposite. Something has happened to boys who no longer use their school performance to feel good about themselves. What's more, if your teachers do not know you, like you, respect you, understand you, or fail to bond with you, disidentifying with school makes sense. Would you want to stay in a place where you're feared or not liked? The fact that Black boys do not value academics means we have failed to integrate their culture into school culture. We have failed to enter into their world. If Black boys do not resonate with school culture, they will not connect self-esteem with academic proficiency. We need a sense of urgency and passion; we need workshops, conferences, and more discussions about this significant schism between self-esteem and school-esteem, Black male culture and school culture.

Honestly, I commend Black boys for protecting themselves. I get why they have chosen to protect their self-esteem by disidentifying from a negative institution that seems to hate them, refuses to provide books that resonate with them, ignores their learning styles, and suspends them for looking and acting naturally. This defense mechanism makes sense, and it protects them against the disdain and even hatred.

I want to also acknowledge Dr. Jamaal Matthews' dissertation, "Toward a Holistic Understanding of Academic Identification in Ethnic Minority Boys at Risk for Academic Failure." [19] Dr. Matthews points out that belonging, regulation, and values are needed for boys to identify with school. Let's review these in detail.

Belonging. Dr. Matthews says that if we want Black boys to identify with school and connect self-esteem to school-esteem, educators must make them feel they belong. Earlier, I mentioned the principal of Booker T. Washington High School in Memphis who is requiring that her teachers love the students. This makes students feel special and important. Many Black boys dropped out because they felt no one would miss them.

Interestingly, décor can help Black boys feel important in school. Do you have pictures of Black males in the main corridor, cafeteria, gymnasium, and classroom? Do these locations feature displays of meaningful quotes from African American males? Are African American male characters in the stories the students must read? Is your library stocked with books that are of interest to African American males? Do you have any Black male teachers, teacher assistants, and mentors in your school?

Morehouse, the only African American male college in America, has monthly convocations, or assemblies, that inspire Black males. If you want to help Black boys identify with school and help them connect self-esteem and school-esteem, weekly or monthly convocations that feature guest speakers and mentors can be very useful.

Regulation. Dr. Matthews documents that for African American males to be successful, they must learn how to regulate themselves. They must understand how work connects to achievement. For example, do your boys know that Ray Allen of the Miami Heat practices hundreds of jump shots every day? We have to help Black boys understand that to do well academically, you have to discipline, or regulate yourself. There's a correlation between your work ethic and being on the honor roll. Doing well in school depends on how well you regulate yourself. We must teach Black males the secret of success: Whatever you do most is what you do best.

Values. Your values determine how you conduct your life. What do our boys value? Where do they learn their values? It is clear that for the most part, they do not value academics, but we must make our case about how academics can lead to a prosperous life. We must teach African American males to value academics.

One way to do this is simple math. Discuss how much, on average, high school dropouts, ($8) high school graduates ($12), college graduates ($24), and graduates with master's and doctorate degrees ($48) will earn per hour or annually. African American males are not convinced that education is financially worthwhile. They believe the odds are better in sports, music, and crime. To help them develop a strong connection between self-esteem and school-esteem, Black male culture and school culture, we must build a strong qualitative and quantitative case for the financial value of education.

I often ask male students, "Will you make more money as a teacher or drug dealer?" Almost 100 percent of the audience believes a drug dealer earns more money. We must be able to convince Black boys that ultimately teachers earn more than drug dealers—and they have a longer life span.

We must also take a serious look at Black boys' assumption that being smart is acting White. In separate publications, Stuart Buck and Roland Fryer write about the quantitative and qualitative impact of acting White on the development of peer group connections among Black and Hispanic male students who are pursuing high academic achievement. Both authors observe that the higher the GPA was for Black male students, the more friends they lost—at a rate of seven times the rate of friends lost among White male students earning high GPAs. In other words, when White male students earned high academic marks they experienced a corresponding rise in popularity; the opposite was the case among high achieving African American male students.[20]

In my book, *To Be Popular or Smart: The Black Peer Group,* we looked at this idea that being smart is acting White. It is very difficult for Black males to do well in school when the peer group associates being smart with Whites. An improved school culture for African American males will reinforce the idea that being smart is acting Black. We must reinforce this idea every day, every hour on the hour. In addition, we must convince them that being smart is acting masculine.

Buck discusses how before Brown vs. Topeka and integration, in highly concentrated African American schools, Black children did not associate being smart with acting White. It is difficult to attend a school that is 50 percent White, 50 percent Black, and the White students are on the second floor in advanced classes and the Black students are on the first floor in regular, remedial, and special education classes. Now imagine you're the only Black student on the second floor while all your friends are on the first. Is it any wonder why some boys resist being placed in advanced classes?

Chapter 13: Peer Group Culture

Black boys find that once in these classes, some teachers, who do not look like them, seem to question whether they should even be there. Their friends tease and accuse them of acting White. Many Black females seem to value the ball player over the scholar. An African American mother once told me that her son, who was in fifth grade at the time, was teased by an eighth-grade male for "talking White." The eighth grader made her son talk again in front of his friends, and they all had a good laugh at her son's expense. That's the kind of experience that can influence a boy for life. To fit in and be accepted by his peers, this young male began a downward slide into poor grades, poor classroom behavior, and low school- and self-esteem. We must "hack" the Black male peer group to change this erroneous notion that being smart is acting White and feminine.

An excellent writing assignment would be to have your boys discuss and write about the smartest people they know. Do not censor them, because they may cite a gangbanger or drug dealer. What we want them to analyze is why they are smart. What constitutes being smart? Then have them list and write about five Black men from African American or African history, who were geniuses in medicine, science, technology, mathematics, and the arts. A follow-up assignment could focus your boys on the same subjects (the five smartest people they know and the five Black men from history), examining this time on how these smart—and maybe not-so-smart—men seemed to have overcome something in their lives in order to demonstrate their intelligence. The aim of the follow-up assignment is for your boys to discover through their own analysis how obstacles are commonplace for the smart and the not-so-smart alike; it depends on how a person approaches obstacles that can make a critical difference.

In the chapter on racism, we will discuss Post-Traumatic Slavery Disorder, which has, in no small way, affected our understanding of intelligence. Associating being smart with acting White clearly illustrates the impact that racism has had on the lives of our boys. You won't find a White student on the honor roll being teased and accused of acting Black. Why don't White students associate being smart with acting Black?

Many African American students attend schools where the curriculum is Eurocentric. When children are taught that Columbus did not discover America, that Lincoln did not free the slaves, that Egypt is not in the Middle East, and that Imhotep, not Hippocrates, is the father of medicine, they will no longer associate being smart with acting White.

The good news is that you can overcome Post-Traumatic Slavery Disorder when you know your culture and history. That's why the message of this book is so important—we must change the culture of both African American males and school. One way to do this is to make the curriculum more multicultural and Africentric.

One of the many things my oldest son and I have in common was that we were both in honors classes during our school years, and we both attempted to walk the fence between school culture and Black male culture. It was okay to be in honors if you didn't study. Or it's okay to be in honors if you're also a ball player. The real challenge for African American males who are in honors classes is, as Dr. Matthews stated, regulation or self-discipline. It's difficult getting an A in algebra, geometry, and trigonometry, biology, chemistry, and physics without studying. It may be possible in third grade to get an A on a test without studying, but it becomes more difficult to earn an A in the intermediate, upper, and high school grades.

African American males who are trying to walk the fence have a difficult decision to make. Do they take the book home and study for the test and risk ridicule from friends, or do they take a chance and not study? How many engineers, doctors, computer programmers, accountants, and scholars have we lost because the peer group won this battle?

Another way of walking the fence is to be in honors classes and also play ball, dance, fight, or rap. At some point, though, life will force you to choose. You can't always divide your time equally. When I attended Illinois State University, there were 1,000 Black freshmen, but only 246 of us graduated four years later. It wasn't necessarily because we were smarter. It's because we realized that at some point you have to leave the cafeteria and the student lounge, you have to stop playing cards and ball, and you have to go to your dormitory room or the library and study.

Schools teach more than the three R's. There is a hidden, middle-class, Eurocentric curriculum that promotes middle-class values and teaches students to value individualism, competition, and White supremacy and Eurocentric culture.

Sometimes I take my grandson swimming, and there in the pool I see other White children playing the game Marco Polo. So I changed the name of that game, and my grandson and I now play Martin King and Malcolm X, but not Marco Polo.

There are other ways the hidden curriculum is taught. Most schools have academic assembly programs. There may be 300 students or more in the auditorium, yet the principal and teachers only give one to five awards. The emphasis is on the minority, not the majority. That goes against African culture, communalism, cooperation, and the value of "we." If you're only going to acknowledge one to five students during the assembly, there's a very good chance that African American male students are not going to buy into academic achievement because you've left out their peers.

I've heard horror stories where African American males have pleaded with their teachers and principals, "Please do not give me an award in front of my peer group. Just give it to me after school. I'll put it in my book bag, but I don't want anyone to know that I received an award." Most boys do not want to be publicly complimented by their teachers because of the teasing they know they will receive from peers. When we successfully change school culture, public praise will become acceptable. Even better, the cooperative groups will receive the praise.

I recommend the Nguzo Saba Assembly Program. If you have 300 students in the audience, most if not all should receive an award. If a student moves from a D to a C, he receives an award. If a student moves from a C to an A, he receives two awards. This way there's a potential chance that a much larger number than one to five are going to receive an award, and just maybe we'll be able to use the peer group to inspire academic achievement. Just maybe in the Nguzo Saba Assembly Program, Black boys will appear more comfortable with receiving awards. If we want to change school culture for African American males, these are the types of strategies and programs schools need to implement.

When I was in sixth grade, I received 100 on a math test. My teacher asked me what my best friend Darryl received. I snickered, and she didn't like that. She asked me to bring my paper to her desk. Then she asked me one last time to tell her the grade Darryl received. I said, "40." She then drew an X through my 100 and wrote 40. Now if you value "I" over "we," you don't like this story. But she was trying to teach me more than just math. She was trying to teach me how to be a blessing to someone else. Her curriculum was different from the Eurocentric curriculum. Hers promoted "we" and not "I," cooperation and not competition. Darryl and I formed a buddy group. Some teachers prefer a buddy group over a group of five. They feel it's easier to manage, less movement and noise.

In a cooperative learning environment, students will learn how to respect and appreciate each other. The A students will learn patience with struggling students. Struggling students will learn to respect the A students. In fact, the ridicule that A students often face should decrease given their enhanced value in a cooperative learning environment. As captain of the team, they will be valued.

A fraternity was pledging some new recruits, and there were 10 students on line. Only one of the students knew the information. So when they were tested, the leader found out that only one knew the information.

He had the other nine paddle the one student who knew. Unfortunately, the one student had been operating under the premise that "I" was more important than "we." The leader was trying to promote that everyone needs to know the information, and we can't keep knowledge to ourselves for selfish reasons.

"A study published in the journal *Cognition and Instruction* [by Dr. Wade Boykin] finds that black students in fourth and fifth grades perform better academically than certain types of learning environments....In the study researchers divided a large group of fourth- and fifth-graders at an urban school in the Northeast and placed them in three different learning environments. One group was placed in a communal learning environment where they were urged to work together to solve problems. A second group was told they would earn an award if the combined performance of the group exceeded expectations. The third group was told that those individuals who performed the best would be rewarded. The results showed that black students performed best in the communal group. The black students showed the worst performance in the third group that emphasized individual achievement. White students, on the other hand, performed the best in the group that emphasized individual competition and did the worst in the communal group."[21]

These findings are highly significant. Cooperative learning is effective and congruent with the values, spirit, and nature of African American children, yet we continue to subject Black boys to a classroom based on the individualism and competitiveness of White culture. We no longer need to try to make African American males European and achieve academic excellence through individual effort. African American males no longer need to worry about appearing to act White or feminine if they do well in school. They should not have to make the agonizing choice of advanced classes or their friends. Why not have five African American males in honors classes together? The research shows that when Black students study together as a group, academic performance is improved. **Cooperative learning needs to be a cornerstone of our new and improved school culture.**

Black boys do everything together except study. They play ball together, they play the dozens together, they eat together, they play video games together, they dance together, they have fun together. Everything they do in the gymnasium, the cafeteria, their homes, and the community, they do together. Yet in the classroom, they are separated. This is a clear indication that Black male culture has not integrated into school culture. We are still living in two separate and distinct cultures.

Now let's boost the effectiveness of cooperative learning even more by using the innate competitiveness of boys. It may seem paradoxical, but Black boys are both cooperative and competitive. They can work together in a group, and then compete as a unit against other groups. This dynamic will turbo-boost learning and greatly improve school culture for your boys.

We know that girls mature faster than boys, but maybe that's because we haven't yet figured out how to tap into the innate strengths of boys. One of those strengths is teamwork. One of the best ways to maximize academic achievement is to have boys compete against girls. If you want to see Black boys at their finest, have them work together in a group and then compete against girls. In a single gender classroom, they will compete among each other. You will be amazed at their improved performance working in groups while competing against each other.

Another tool to use in your cooperative learning kit is *time.* Boys understand time well because in many sports, like basketball, football, and even video games, timing increases the energy and competitive spirit of the game. Break down certain tasks and give your boys only a certain time to complete them. Have repetitive writing, reading, and vocabulary drills performed under tight and exciting time constraints. Conduct the drills with great flourish: use a flag or sound a buzzer. Make a great show of constantly looking at your stopwatch. Make learning fun!

If you don't do anything else give cooperative learning a try—and don't give up after a day or a week. Try it for the entire school year. I think you'll be pleasantly surprised. But beware; learning in groups can get noisy. Just realize that the process is working. Monitor the groups to ensure they are debating about the task at hand. Don't let them go off on tangents. As an added incentive, let students know that the groups that do the best work will receive a really nice award (not a dictionary or pen). I've seen this work wonders in many schools. Self-esteem and school-esteem, Black male culture and school culture are being stitched seamlessly together. Black males begin to take for granted that being smart is acting Black and masculine. You will succeed at breaking down the erroneous assumptions that have long held Black male students at the bottom of every academic indicator.

Writing Assignment
Have your boys write about their closest male friend and why they are best friends. What is the difference between a friend and an associate?

Have boys write about intelligence. Would they rather be cool or smart? A scholar or a basketball player? Is being smart acting White? Is being smart acting feminine? How do your friends feel about nerds? Have them write about cooperative learning groups.

In the next chapter, we will look at sports culture.

Chapter 14: Sports Culture

Kicking off with sports, the next few chapters will examine the major influences on Black males, including rap, gangs, television, video games, drugs, prison, sexuality, and fatherlessness. It is so unfortunate that Black boys can live in a world with so many challenges, and their school and curriculum do not provide the resources to address these challenges.

Sports are near and dear to the hearts of Black males, and sports can be used as a force for good. Our 10-year-old grandson loves to read and is very good at math, but one day he told my wife and I that there's nothing he enjoys more than playing basketball. He said he could play basketball every day.

What is it about sports that have captured the imagination of Black males so much?

In the excellent book *"Multiplication Is for White People": Raising Expectations for Other People's Children,* Lisa Delpit shares the following insight:

> "He comes back because it's fun: it is engaging because he uses his mind and his body; he can monitor his own progress, adjusting his attempts to match his assessment; It is connected to his interests. He comes back so that he can be part of a culturally rewarding community activity: he wants to get the praise of his peers; his entire community supports basketball; he wants to fit in. He comes back because he believes he can get better: he knows that people who look like him have been successful; he sees this success on television and his own community. He comes back because he believes he might get financially rewarded for getting better: he sees people on television who look like him get high salaries for being good at basketball."[22]

Let's dissect this quote.

He comes back because it's fun. If we want to successfully change school culture for Black males, we need to make language arts, reading, social studies, science, and math fun. Once of the best ways to make school subjects fun is to make them culturally relevant and teach in a way that's complementary to their learning styles. One of the best ways to bore students is to teach a concept that is culturally irrelevant and in a pedagogy that's not conducive to their learning styles.

He uses his mind and his body. Unfortunately, tactile and kinesthetic learners seldom if ever use their bodies from the fourth grade on. If we want to understand the world of Black boys, we need to understand the synergy between mind and body. Boys are sitting unnaturally still for long periods of time during the school day. This is unhealthy, promotes obesity, and is only conducive to boredom and fatigue. Some schools use recess and gym as forms of punishment—in other words, if boys don't behave, they don't get gym or recess. Yet if gym and recess were mandatory, regardless of behavior, teachers would probably see behavior improve. It's as if we do not want the body to be involved in the school day. We should have as many classes outside as weather permits. Boys love classes outside.

He wants to get the praise of his peers. Does your school provide more praise for athletes or scholars? Basketball and football teams receive big trophies, but the debate teams and science fair winners receive little buttons or a ribbon that says "WINNER." Accolades given to NFL and NBA athletes in the media are exciting, but schools are also guilty of acknowledging and giving more accolades to athletes than to scholars.

Let's give our scholars big trophies, massive assemblies with loud music and praise. Let's have pep rallies for scholars before a big competitive event. They should know their school supports them. This is positive, optimistic school culture in action. Have live drummers and dancers perform for the Nguzo Saba assembly program, where awards and praise will be given to groups, not just individuals. Giving praise to the peer group empowers educators to effectively influence Black males with positive values, ideas, and behaviors.

He comes back because he believes he can get better. The motto of Urban Prep Academy in Chicago is "We believe." It is difficult to do well in any endeavor if you do not believe. Attitude is critical to success, and that includes the attitude of both educators and students. Unfortunately, many Black boys believe they are better in sports than in science, music than math, rap than reading. One reason why they believe this is because the expectations of their teachers are low. Boys thrive with Master Teachers who believe, "You will learn, and I can teach!" When teachers subscribe to Rule 110, that spirit permeates throughout the entire classroom. After being retained and being forced to read in the same time span as girls, along with all the other problems we've discussed thus far, many Black

Chapter 14: Sports Culture

boys do not believe that school is going to be effective for them. They actually believe as early as fourth grade that they have a better chance of going pro in the NBA than becoming a doctor, engineer, computer programmer, or accountant.

That's why the convocations held at Morehouse College and other HCBUs are so important. If students 18 to 25 years of age still need to be motivated, encouraged, and instilled with the belief that they can do well, surely elementary, junior high, and high school students need the same.

[There are] people who look like him. Earlier, I mentioned the important of décor. Unfortunately, classrooms from the fourth grade on have such a drab décor that live children die in those classrooms. Our boys are excited, motivated, and inspired by the images of LeBron James, Dwyane Wade, Kevin Durant, Derrick Rose, and Kobe Bryant. Remember, our boys need to see themselves paired next to images of their heroes on the walls of their schools and classrooms. Our boys see Black ball players all the time.

Can you name 5 Black doctors, Black lawyers, Black engineers, Black accountants, and Black scholars? If you can't, there's a good chance your students can't, either. This would be a good research and writing assignment for both you and your students.

He comes back because he believes he might get financially rewarded. Our boys believe they can make more at almost every endeavor other than education. They even believe they can make more money selling drugs than they can by using their education. We must convince Black boys that there's an educational payoff. We must let them know that if you make $25,000 per year times 40 years, that's $1 million. If you make $50,000 per year times 40 years, that's $2 million. Our boys need to be exposed to that kind of information.

I have visited schools where 200 Black boys have tried out for 12 slots on the basketball team. You do the math. They knew going into this endeavor that 188 of them were not going to make it. But because of their love of sports, especially basketball, and the fact that they believed in themselves enough, they tried to make the team against all odds. One of the most important aspects of life is to believe in yourself, to try and pursue your desires and goals. Why is it that so few African American males would try out for the debate team or the science fair team?

Michael Jordan has said that he's taken the game-winning shot more than 300 times and missed more than two-thirds of them. But he was never reluctant to take the last shot. He believed in himself enough to take the last shot. He said he wasn't afraid to fail. In sports, Black boys are not afraid to fail. They are willing to try out for the team, knowing only 12 of 200 are going to make it. Even more significantly, they're not afraid to fail in front of their peer group. Why are they not afraid to fail in front of their peers when playing ball, but cannot bear the idea of giving a wrong answer in class? The peer group endorses sports, and so it's acceptable to fail in sports as long as you show up and try hard. The peer group has decided that sports, especially basketball is something that Black males do well.

We must develop the same strong belief, spirit, and confidence in Black males for academics. We must teach them that if they try out for AP, gifted, and talented classes, the science fair, and debate team but don't make it, that's okay. It's okay because Africans were the first to develop the principles of math and science, the first to build pyramids and civilization, and our boys have that DNA within them. If they didn't make it the first time, with study and determination, they can and will succeed. This is the way to get the peer group to endorse science, math, and scholarship. They have to understand that the genius is already within them. In the spirit of *educere*, it is your job as educators to draw that brilliance out of them.

Ask your male students if they believe they can go pro in the NBA. Then show them the following chart:

- 1 million high school boys try out for their high school team.
- 400,000 make the high school team.
- 4,000 make the college team.
- 35 make it to the NBA.
- 7 start.
- The average career in the NBA lasts 4 years (3 years for the NFL).

Talk to your boys about the statistical possibility of joining the NBA. If there are one million African American males trying out for seven full-time jobs that only last four years, what are their chances of success? Then show them the following:

- There are 100,000 jobs available for engineers.
- Less than 2,000 African American males qualify.
- The average career lasts 40 years and pays $100,000 per year ($4 million).

We don't want to discourage Black boys from pursuing their dreams in the NBA, NFL, and other sports, but we do want to give them a balanced perspective. In fact, encourage their pursuit of sports. Excellent athletic skills can help pay their way through college through scholarships. However, let them know that the wisest athletes get degrees that will help them long after athletic ability and interest have faded away. For example, according to BET.com, the following African American pro athletes received valuable college degrees that will continue to make them marketable after their pro ball careers have ended:

- Shaquille O'Neal – received his doctorate degree in education in 2012 and is interested in obtaining a law degree
- Vince Carter – bachelor's degree in African American studies, University of North Carolina
- Tim Duncan – bachelor's degree in psychology, Wake Forest University
- John Mayberry, Jr– bachelor's degree in political science, Stanford University
- Usama Young – bachelor's degree in educational studies, Kent State University
- Matt Forte – bachelor's degree in finance, Tulane University

Robert Griffin III, quarterback for the Washington Redskins, is one of my favorite scholar-athletes. He's known for his speed and aim on the football field and, among many awards, winning the Heisman Trophy in 2011 and the Associated Press NFL Offensive Rookie of the Year award in 2012. However, his achievements began earlier.. He was president of his senior class in high school, ranked seventh in his class, graduated early, started college at 17 years of age, received his bachelor's degree in political science *in three years* with a 3.67 GPA, and was working on his master's degree in communications when the NFL came calling. Griffin not only played college football, he ran track and advanced to the semifinals in the U.S. Olympic trials. If that weren't enough, he was on the Dean's List not once but twice during his college career.

Griffin's two major influences? His father and his faith in God. He said, "I was heavily influenced by my parents to learn discipline. But my relationship with God was my most important influence."

Although Griffin is undoubtedly a gifted athlete, it's his dedication to scholarship that interests me. Ask your students what their options are if they don't become professional athletes. Have them research and name 10 professional ball players who have degrees from universities. Have them list the top 10 schools for Black athletes, and the lowest 10 schools in terms of their Black male graduation rate.

Ever heard of March Madness? During the month of March, the top 64 college basketball teams compete for the national championship. While the schools are 95 percent White, the basketball teams are almost 95 percent African American. Have your students discuss this and explain these extreme numbers.

Then we have May Sadness. Every year the universities made *millions* of dollars during March Madness, but the athletes receive nothing. What's worse, in May, many Black male students do not graduate. Less than one-third of Black college players graduate from college. Please share with your students that 60 percent of NBA players and 78 percent of NFL players are bankrupt after five years of retirement from professional sports. Have your students discuss how players can earn $5 million or more per year for four years and five years later are bankrupt.[23]

I also want you to ask your students why athletes are paid more than teachers. Why are athletes paid more than police officers and firefighters? Why do athletes get paid more than almost any other profession?

Have students list sports other than basketball and football, then discuss the possibility of playing other sports. Explain to your boys that there's a greater chance of getting a scholarship playing second base in baseball, being a left-handed relief pitcher, joining the swim, tennis, or golf teams, especially at an HBCU, than getting a basketball or football scholarship.

Discuss work ethic with your boys. Do they spend more time studying or playing sports? Whatever they do most will be what they do best. One of the reasons why Ray Allen is the leader of three-point shooting is because he has a well-known, daily routine of practices that exceeds what most other players . Try to convince your boys that if they spent that much time reading and studying, they would increase their chances of becoming a scholar, engineer, doctor, or any other high paying career professional.

Have your boys write about the following issues:
- Why are the NBA and NFL the most popular sports among Black males?
- How do you feel about football players getting concussions? How will that impact their long-term health?
- Write a letter to your favorite player.
- Write a letter to your favorite team's coach, and give him some advice.
- Research and write a report about how Magic Johnson transformed himself from an NBA All-Star to a multimillionaire entrepreneur.

Chapter 14: Sports Culture

- Research and write a report about Michael Jordan now owning an NBA team.
- Write about all the non-playing positions that are available on a sports team, especially in the NBA.
- Solve the following math problems:
  - A basketball player took 12 three-point shots and made four. What is his percentage?
  - A basketball player scored 25 points. Give five examples of how he could have scored them. Extra credit for the most ways they scored.
  - A football team scored 35 points. Give examples of how they could have scored.

Create a budget for a ball player who earns $5 million per year, and at the end of the year is broke. Create another budget and show how four years later he has more than when he started.

A closely related topic to sports is gym shoes. Designer gym shoes are extremely important to Black males. Writing Assignment

Have your students write a short story based on the following statement: "Before I let anyone take my gym shoes, they will have to kill me."

Discuss why they feel so strongly about their gym shoes. Why would Black males risk their lives over gym shoes?

What is the effect gym shoes have on their self-esteem?

Why would a boy from a low-income family spend close to $300 for a pair of gym shoes? Why would gym shoe manufacturers sell shoes for $300 that only cost them $5 to make with cheap overseas labor? (Pop math quiz: What does "markup" mean? What is the markup in this scenario?)

How does it make you feel to wear the new Air Jordan shoes? How does it feel to wear the latest gym shoe?

Have you or a friend ever had a fight about gym shoes? Explain the circumstances around the fight. How do you feel about it now?

Name the athletes who are selling less expensive shoes and have expressed concern about the amount of money and violence that has occurred around more expensive gym shoes. How do you feel about those athletes and the position they have taken? Would you wear their shoes? Why or why not?

Have students write a letter to Michael Jordan, LeBron James, and any other athlete who is connected with an expensive shoe line around which this violence occurs.

In the next chapter, we will delve deeply into the world of Black males and rap culture.

Chapter 15: Rap Culture

The second greatest influence on Black male youth is rap music. If we want to go into their world and understand it and try to connect school culture with their culture, what is your school doing about connecting your curriculum to hip hop culture and rap music? There is such a disconnection between what has the hearts and minds of Black males and what they are exposed to in school.

There should be a wealth of material in language arts and social studies that we could draw upon to connect the curriculum and hip hop/rap culture. For example, one of the more popular shows on BET is *106 & Park*. This daily show covers the top 10 rap videos of the week and is very popular, especially among African American males. Language arts teachers want students to master spelling, expand their vocabulary, and improve their reading and writing skills. If *106 & Park* has the hearts and minds of students and you want to teach reading, vocabulary, spelling, and writing, why not bring in the television version of rap music and videos, where there's no profanity, and either play the CD or video.

Of the top 10 videos of the week, you choose one per day. Have students listen or watch the video then write down all the words in the video. Check for spelling. These are the vocabulary words for the week. You can also have students write an analysis of the video. This will improve their reading comprehension, writing and critical thinking skills. They would rather listen to 106 & Park than your lecture.

Social studies and history teachers, have your students write a paper on the history of hip hop. What changes have occurred in rap lyrics from the early 1980s to the present? When hip hop first started, groups created both dance music and message music. One of Public Enemy's most famous and powerful songs, first released in 1989 was "Fight the Power." Have your students listen to that CD and discuss what Public Enemy was trying to convey.

Gil Scott Heron in the 1994 CD *Message to the Messengers* challenged today's rappers. He wondered how in one song a rapper calls a female a queen and on the same album, different track, a rapper calls her a b–. Which one is she? Have your students discuss this.

The tune "Can't Leave Him Alone" was done by 50 Cent and Ciara and released in 2007. The lyrics say, "I tried that good boy game, but that dope boy is turning me on." Have your students discuss what the artists are trying to convey in this song. Are these lyrics successful in shaping the minds of youth? Other writing assignments and topics for discussion are as follows:

- Have students list their five favorite rappers and explain why they like them.
- Have them list five rappers who write positive, nonviolent lyrics.
- Have them list five rappers who write negative, violent lyrics.
- Ask them if they think there's a greater chance of securing a rap contract and receiving radio airplay with positive or negative lyrics.
- Ask them if they think music labels are controlling the minds of Black youth.
- Ask them if they think radio stations are controlling the minds of Black youth.
- Have them write letters to EMI, BMG, Time Warner, and Universal, complaining about the scarcity of positive lyrics and positive rappers being signed and promoted.
- In hip hop and rap culture, one of the contributing factors to fighting and the suspension rate are the rifts between rappers. Have students read and write about Tupac and Biggie, Lil JoJo and Chief Keef, Jay-Z and Nas, 50 Cent and Ja Rule, Lil Wayne and Pusha T, Game and Shyne, 50 Cent and Floyd Mayweather, Common and Drake, MC Hammer and Jay-Z, 50 Cent and Rick Ross, and Drake and Chris Brown. Have them provide five more current rifts that are taking place in the hip hop world. What caused the rift? Is it worth people being shot and killed over the rift?
- Many youth believe that rap lyrics do not affect their view of the world. They believe they are only into the beat. Ask your students to write down the last song they heard before they came into school. Their brain, which is similar to a computer, will probably play throughout the day the last song they heard before they entered school. Unfortunately, some teachers allow the sleepers and quiet students to play their iPods in class as long as they do not disturb the other students. This is simply unacceptable.
- Have a discussion with your youth about the "N" word. Discuss the difference between spellings: "nigger" and "nigga." Have them discuss the "N" word as if they were having a conversation with Frederick Douglass and Harriet Tubman. Have them explain how it's okay for a Black youth to use the "N" word with each other, but it's not acceptable for a White person to say it to them. Ultimately, what you're trying to get across is the power of words. If you are a writer, singer, poet, or communicator, all you have are your words.
- Discuss saggin', which is "niggas" spelled backwards. In prison, inmates are not allowed to wear belts, and this is the origin of saggin'. Adults tell students that if they want to get a job in Corporate America, they must speak standard English and dress in corporate

attire. The reality is that many Black males don't want to work in Corporate America. They'd rather follow ball players and rappers who are splitting verbs and saggin' all the way to the bank.

- Discuss tattoos with your students. Are they safe? What are some negative consequences? Is it appropriate to tattoo a large portion of your body? Will it affect your ability to get a job in Corporate America? Do you care? What types of tattoos are popular among Black male youth?

Now look at some of those videos on *106 & Park* within the context of the "N" word, saggin', and tattoos. These videos are about more than lyrics. They are promoting a lifestyle that is very attractive to Black males. If we're going to change the culture for Black males, we must compete and not back away from the negative impact rappers and hip hop culture are having on Black male youth.

Some adults, both parents and educators, are silent about these lyrics and videos. Black males are watching and listening to these lyrics with little input from adults. As a result, they are being highly influenced by rappers.

One single mother, a friend of mine, once told me that when she was raising her two children, a boy and a girl, during the height of the gangsta rap era, she felt like she was competing against hip hop and rap culture. She felt like she was standing alone against a great cultural tidal wave that had consumed her children. If the radio was on while they were in the car, inevitably a gangsta rap tune with negative lyrics got airtime. The son decided he wanted to be a rapper and went around the house freestyling and battling with his friends. The daughter loved dancing to the music. Rap music seemed to always be in the atmosphere.

This mother decided to fight fire with fire. Whenever a gangsta rap tune came on the radio, whenever she heard one of them spitting lyrics in the house, she called them on it. She wouldn't make her children stop listening or rapping. She knew they'd only listen outside of the house, and she wanted to influence their perceptions around the music. So instead, she had them repeat the lyrics and then explain what they meant. She then shared, in great detail, how the lyrics went against the family's values. She asked them, "Would you want your own children listening to this? How would you feel if your daughter was a dancer in a rap video? How would you feel if your child called your wife a b–? Should you really be dancing to lyrics that promote drug use and violence against women?" Of course they said the lyrics meant nothing, they were just into the beat. Then this mother explained how the beat was being used to program their minds.

She said, "I challenged my children every time I had the opportunity, which was pretty much on a daily basis. It became my mission in life to defuse the impact this music had on their minds. I got on their nerves, but I didn't care about that. I felt I was fighting for their sanity and the sanctity of our family's values."

This mother never missed an opportunity to "hack" the music. She was relentless. Today, as young adults, they still love rap and hip hop, but they mostly enjoy more positive lyrics that fuel the underground culture of rap, the rap tunes that never receive airtime on the radio or *106 & Park*. Her son has become quite a prolific writer of rap lyrics in the spirit of Gil Scott and Public Enemy, and her daughter often accompanies poets at spoken word events with her cello. This mother told me, "Mission accomplished."

In your language arts classes, have students write a hip hop song. Have them write lyrics that are positive; then have them write negative lyrics. Ask them which ones they like. Which song would sell? Have them stand up in front of the class and recite, in the style of spoken word, their lyrics. This assignment will help improve their writing and public speaking skills. It is amazing to me how many teachers feel that Black males lack communication skills. Yet if you give them an opportunity to recite their own rhymes in the spirit of spoken word, they will shine. I encourage weekly spoken word contests. I also suggest you expose your students to the excellent spoken word off You Tube titled, "Why I Hate School but Love Education

It is difficult for me to speak about topics that don't interest me. But if you give me a topic that I'm passionate about, something that I wrote and feel strongly about, I come alive. We will improve school culture when we begin to include their world.

Last but not least, the following are word problems that math teachers can use to challenge their boys.

- If you sell one million CDs at $18 each, how much will you earn?
- Distributors make 50 percent from each CD. We have one million CDs that cost $18 each, totaling $18 million. How much will distributors earn? The producers make 40 percent. How much will they earn? The cost of the video and CD was $800,000. There's $1 million left—but wait. The IRS takes 50 percent. How much went to the IRS? How much is left?
- What would a Black male buy? Probably buy a car. What type?
- Less than 10 percent of rappers make more than $100,000.
- Almost 90 percent of all rappers are struggling financially to make ends meet.
- The houses and cars that you see in the videos on *106 & Park* were rented by the studio for filming the videos, not for the rappers to reside. Only 10 percent of rappers own the houses and cars that you see in the videos.

In the next chapter, we will look at television and video game culture.

Chapter 16: Television and Video Game Culture

The third greatest influence on Black male youth are television and video games.

- African American males watch 38 hours of television per week.
- Two-thirds of all programs contain violence:
  - 200,000 violent acts
  - 16,000 murders
- Youth view 14,000 sexual scenes, 90 percent of which are outside of marriage.
- Youth see 2,000 ads for beer and wine.[24]

Thirty-eight hours of watching television is a lot of hours. Black boys spend more time watching television than they spend in school, and the influence of television is far greater than school. If television has captured the minds of our youth, we need to go into their world and have an honest discussion about these 200,000 violent acts, 16,000 murders, and 14,000 sexual scenes.

In 2013, the most violent shows were *Spartacus* (25 deaths per hour), *Game of Thrones, Nikita, The Walking Dead,* and *Oz.* Ask your students for their five favorite TV shows and why they watch those shows. Have them write a paper about each show.

As educators, our objective is to develop and improve students' writing and critical thinking skills. We want them to be able to analyze, dissect, and debate the issues. Why don't we draw from what they enjoy watching and have that be a focal point of the curriculum in language arts? As we not only improve language arts skills, we empower them to better understand what they're watching.

Let's have an honest discussion with youth about the significance of advertising. Most corporations believe their best markets are adolescents. A 30-second commercial during the Super Bowl will cost almost $4 million. Why would Nike spend $4 million for 30 seconds if they were not absolutely sure that their ideal market, Black male adolescents, would spend $200 or more for a pair of gym shoes that only cost $5? The reality is that Nike spends more money to advertise the shoe than to make the shoe. They know their advertising will lead to big profits.

Bring in ads from magazines or tapes of television commercials and have students discuss if they thought the ads were influential. Do the ads make people buy? Have them explain their answers.

One reason why there are so many ads promoting beer and wine is because manufacturers know that if they can get an adolescent to drink (or smoke), they will have this consumer for the next 20 to 30 years or until they die from using the products. We must help Black male youth understand that decisions made as adolescents determine the quality of their lives as adults.

The ultimate objective of this chapter is for educators to understand the following:

1. Black male youth watch more television than any other youth in America.
2. Television has a tremendous influence on their lives.
3. Television has captured their interest and imagination.
4. There's no connection between what they watch on television and what they discuss in school.
5. Many Black male youth are watching television without any adult input and discussion.

This needs to change, especially if we're going to successfully change school culture for Black males.

Video Games
African American males play about 21 hours of video games per week.[25] In 2013, the most violent games were:

- Resident Evil
- Grand Theft Auto
- God of War
- Narc
- Killer7
- The Warriors
- 50 Cent: Bulletproof
- Crime Life Gang Wars
- Call of Duty
- Postal

Chapter 16: Television and Video Game Culture

- Mortal Kombat
- Manhunt
- Splatterhouse
- MadWorld

Have your students discuss these video games. Do they play them? Have students name their top five video games and why they like them. Then have them write a paper on each of their favorite video games.

Many educators try to convince me that Black males have short attention spans. I think we need to qualify that statement. They may have a short attention span for Shakespeare, Columbus, Lincoln and Hippocrates and any other subject that is not interesting to them, but if you give Black boys a book, rap CD, television, or video game that they enjoy, they can stay focused for 21 hours.

We must acknowledge their interest in video games and use this as a catalyst to improve their writing and other language arts skills. We must connect Black male culture to school culture. Since they have not come into our world, we need to go into theirs. The problem is that we refuse to acknowledge, respect, or understand their world. In fact, we believe they need to come into ours. The dropout rate of almost 50 percent and dismal academic performance of African American males show that our approach is not working. We need to go into their world.

Writing Assignment

Have students name their five favorite websites. Have them write about the content in those websites. Why do they like them? Would they encourage other people to visit those sites?

Ask students if they watch pornography on the Internet. If so, have them list their five favorite pornography sites, and why they like them. Have them describe the content. Do they feel these sites affect their behavior? Later, when we discuss sexuality and fatherlessness, we will discuss the impact of pornography in more detail.

Ask them if they watch YouTube. Have them list their five favorite videos on YouTube and why they like them. Have them write a paper for each video they like.

Teachers, begin to integrate YouTube into your curriculum. You will find that many Black male youth are mesmerized by YouTube.

Ask your students how much time they spend on Facebook, Twitter, and other social media sites. What popular topics and conversations are taking place in social media? Ask them if posting to these sites affects their spelling by having so much of the content in abbreviations and phonetic spellings.

In the next chapter, we will look at the impact of gangs on Black males.

Chapter 17: Gang Culture

For many African American males, their greatest challenge is not algebra, geometry, or trigonometry, biology, chemistry, or physics. Their greatest challenge is the walk from home to school and back. In many instances, it is equally challenging to ride public transit to and from school.

Many educators are clueless about the greatest threats to the safety of African American males. That's why it is so crucial that we take a walk through their neighborhoods. Even parents are not as aware of the gang problem because most drive everywhere. But for young African American males who are not driving, the streets are very dangerous.

Geography teachers, before you discuss the four basic directions and rivers and mountains in other parts of the world, have your students create a map of their neighborhood and indicate which gang controls which territory. Our boys are so fearful that if they make one mistake, it could very well cost them their lives. If they brush up against someone, if they step on someone's gym shoe, if they foul when playing basketball, if there's a rumor that they talked to another male's girlfriend—these behaviors, no matter how innocent in intent, could cost them their lives.

Have your students write down all the reasons why people in their neighborhood fight and kill. Ask them if these reasons make sense. Why would you kill someone over a shoe? Why would you kill someone who brushed up against you or fouled someone during a basketball game? Why would you kill someone who did something in the cafeteria or said something to your girlfriend?

If the threat of violence is the major issue affecting African American males, then how do we help them deal with it? Have Custodians, Referral Agents, and Instructors made a bad situation worse with their lack of empathy and caring?

Have your male students write the names of all the gangs in their neighborhood. This exercise can be done in tandem with history lessons about war or even team battles in sports. Have them describe the hierarchy of the gangs; their history, territories, values, rites, and rituals; and their strengths and weaknesses.

Ask your students if they belong to a gang. What makes gangs so attractive? Some of the reasons why people join gangs are the following:
- Family
- They provide something to do with your time
- Fun
- Protection
- Power
- Money
- Peer pressure
- Male role models

Compare this list to theirs and have them write a paper on each of these reasons for joining a gang.

Have students write about and discuss how they avoid joining gangs.

Have a discussion about the trip home from school and how they avoid coming into contact with gangs.

In certain neighborhoods and schools, only five percent of the students are African American male. In other schools, they are 50 percent or more. Some neighborhoods are more affluent, and there's less gang activity. Other neighborhoods are poor, more dense, predominately African American. So this problem is more acute for some educators and students than others.

Unfortunately, students move from the inner city to the suburbs and bring the gangs and that culture with them. I was very disappointed to learn that some of the leading school districts suspending African American males are in some of the most affluent suburbs. Some school districts with less than 20 percent of African American males were leading the country in suspending Black boys. This problem seems to affect a broad spectrum of African Americans regardless of family income or community type.

Ask your male students to discuss and describe some gang initiations. What's required to join a gang? Do you have to rob someone? Do you have to beat someone? Do you have to kill someone? Do you have to rape someone? Do you have to become an inmate? Once you join, what happens if you change your mind and want to leave?

Is it a coincidence that nationwide, if a student is suspended, more than 70 percent of the time it's a male student? Why are more than 80 percent of homicide victims in the city male? If we don't acknowledge that males are designed to be warriors, protectors, and providers and that they are not going to stay inside the house from 3:00 pm to 10:00 pm for the first 18 years of their lives, if we don't acknowledge that males have a warrior spirit, we will continue to lose them.

Have we designed a female classroom? A female school system? A female culture for male students? Male students are rebelling because of the female culture that exists in schools. Black males need an outlet for their masculine, warrior spirit, and they need to be empowered on how to handle gangs and violence in their neighborhoods.

Not only is there a problem going to and from home and school, but going to the restroom and locker room in some schools can be just as dangerous.

In social studies class, students study the history of wars around the world. Some of the major players in war and creating peace are secretaries of state, prime ministers, governors, and presidents. Let's create lesson plans where we have one group of students representing the gang and another group representing the community. Dissect the issues and have the boys write a paper on what is necessary to create a truce. If possible, have the students send a letter to the gang leaders proposing the truce. There would be nothing better for a Black male who lives in a gang-infested neighborhood than to learn negotiation strategies for creating a gang truce. Since safety is such an issue, why not collaborate with adult male leaders in local businesses, churches, social service agencies, law enforcement, and government agencies to support this effort.

If we could empower Black males in this way, I believe our dropout rate could almost be eliminated. All we have to do is identify the challenges facing our boys and enhance lesson plans in language arts, social studies, math, and science to empower them to deal with what's occurring in their own neighborhoods.

Some Black males have decided that it is safer for them to drop out of school and either stay home or join the gang than to continue to go back and forth between these two worlds that don't communicate, acknowledge, consider, or respect one another.

Ask your boys if they would be interested in sending letters to the police department letting them know where the gangs are and their activities. This is a very sensitive subject. If the boys don't want to do it, we have to respect that. However, don't miss the opportunity to discuss with them why they would not want to do it. In addition to repercussions from gang members, some police officers are on the take. Police officers are often very much aware of where the gangs are, who they are, and what they are doing. Police officers may be on the gang's payroll, which allows gang members to continue their illegal operations uninterrupted. If that's the case, police officers may snitch on any so-called informants to gang leaders. That also needs to be discussed in class.

Educators are usually unaware of the magnitude of this problem. There's a reason why boys do not snitch, why they do not tell school authorities what they know about gangs. There's a reason why our boys do not trust the police. In fact, have your boys discuss and write a paper about whether they trust the police—why or why not? Discuss with your boys racial profiling. Ask them have they been a victim of walking while Black, shopping while Black, standing on corners while Black, and driving while Black. Many police officers act like suspension factories. Have your boys write about how humiliating it is to be frisked.

Schools could reduce the influence of gangs on their students if they reduced the time available to be involved. How can you join a gang if you are involved in extra-curricular activities from 3-6pm and are driven home? If schools provided sports, chess, martial arts, fine arts, debates , science fairs, business contests and other activities on Saturdays how could they join a gang? If schools partnered with churches to program the entire day on Sunday that would also reduce gang influence. Gangs thrive when adults do not program activities for youth.

Guns

While the hidden Eurocentric middle-class curriculum teaches that education is the great equalizer, many Black male youth believe that guns are the great equalizer. Have your boys discuss and write if they believe guns are the great equalizer. Can you take someone's assets and life with a gun? Ask them if they have a gun and how easy it is to get a gun. Have them write a letter to the police department letting them know where guns can be purchased in the neighborhood. Is it necessary to have an automatic weapon in the inner city? What is the purpose of an automatic weapon?

Where in the neighborhood can you learn how to shoot without hitting innocent victims?

Discuss the number of homicides that take place annually in England, Japan, and the United States. According to data gathered for 2012 by the United Nations Office on Drugs and Crime, for the first two countries, it is less than 100. In America, the most violent country in the world, there are more than 20,000 homicides per year. What can America learn from England, Japan, and other countries?

Most of the threat of violence and crime occurs after school, primarily between the hours of 3:00 pm and 6:00 pm. If we could keep Black boys in school during these hours and then provide transportation for them from school to home, we could reduce the danger. The SEED Schools in Baltimore and Washington, DC decided on this approach. In fact, they have created a boarding school experience that extends from Sunday night to Friday evening. I've been honored to speak at the school, and while there I learned that the challenge for students now is from Friday evening to Sunday night. Many boys pray they can survive the mean streets over the weekend. I encourage you to read more about the SEED Schools and the possibility of a SEED School coming to your city.

Writing Assignment

Earlier, we mentioned that one of the reasons people join gangs is because they feel the gang is their family. In traditional families, members take care of one another through sickness and in health. Do your students think gangs function in the same way? Have students discuss and write about what would happen if a gang member got shot. If he became an invalid, would the gang nurse him for the rest of his life? Who would take care of him for the rest of his life? Who would change his underwear? Who would feed him? Who would put on his clothes every morning? Also, do gangs offer medical insurance and disability? Who would pay for treatment and medication for the rest of his life? Who would provide the monthly disability check? The gang? Ask students if they know any gang members currently providing 24-hour, seven-day-a-week nursing home care for an invalid.

In the next chapter, we will look at the impact drugs and prisons have on Black males.

Chapter 18: Drugs/Prison Culture

Are there more Black males in prison, or are there more Black males in college? The media loves telling us how bad things are in the African American community. Most people assume there are more Black males in prison than in college. The reality is that as of 2013 there were 841,000 African American males in prison and 1.4 million in college.

This does not mean things are fine. African Americans are only 13 percent of the U.S. population, but African American males constitute more than 50 percent of the prison population. If you include African American males who are in jail, waiting for trial, and those on parole or probation, the figure then exceeds one million.

The reason why I wanted to combine drugs and prison in this chapter, is because 60 percent of the inmates, whether in jail or prison, on parole or probation, receive their punishment because they were in possession of drugs. In 1980, there were 100,000 African American males involved with the penal institution, but in 2013, there are more than one million African American males involved.

In the early 1980s, the government decided that if you were in possession of five grams of crack, you would receive a mandatory five-year sentence. But, if you were in possession of 499 grams of the original drug, cocaine, you got a slap on the wrist and a warning. This is very similar to schools where a Black male can be suspended because of the way he looks, talks, and maintains eye contact with adults, but for White males to be suspended, they have to possess a gun, knife, or be engaged in a fight that led to bloodshed. There's a parallel between how the penal system and school system distributes punishment.

Have your boys write a paper on crack and cocaine and whether it was fair to have a ratio of 100:1. Ask them why they think Black males were in possession of crack and White males were in possession of cocaine. The government, in their "attempt to be fair," like many schools, reduced the ratio of 100:1 to 18:1. While the disparity is smaller, it still continues to exist. Is this fair? Have them write to the U.S. Department of Justice about this current ratio of 18:1. We could literally reduce the number of African American males who are incarcerated if we simply addressed the issue of drug addiction in America. Have your students research how European countries address drug addiction.

Discuss with your boys what took place in America with regard to prohibition and alcohol. Which drug killed the most Americans last year? Was it cigarettes, alcohol, heroin, or crack cocaine? I'm not going to provide the answer. I want you to research it for yourselves.

Here's a suggestion for a combined social studies and geography assignment. Have your boys draw a map of their neighborhood. Have them identify the locations of liquor stores on the map, then list the stores that sell drug paraphernalia, cigarettes, and liquor to children. Have them write a letter to the mayor and the police department that details the names of the stores that are guilty of these criminal offenses.

Ask students if they've ever smoked a cigarette. Have they ever had alcohol? Have they ever consumed marijuana or any other illegal drug? Have them write about how they felt when they were high. Would they do it again? Have them write a paper on whether heroin, crack and cocaine should be legalized like alcohol was made legal after prohibition. What would be some of the consequences with legalizing heroin, crack and cocaine? Describe what would happen to drivers if these drugs were legalized. Have them discuss and write a paper on whether crack is a best selling product in Black America. How can poor people afford such an expensive habit? What would happen to drug dealers and gangs if crack and cocaine were legalized?

Have students write about whether drug dealers or school teachers make more money.

When do you become a man? Do you become a man when you start smoking? When you start drinking alcohol? When you use illegal drugs? Have students draw a map of their neighborhood and indicate the locations of crack houses. If the students are comfortable doing this, have them write a letter to the police department showing where the crack houses are located.

Throughout this book, we have been looking at the world of young Black males and how various cultures have major impacts on their lives. As influential as the peer group, rap, television, video games, and gangs are, this issue of drugs could be the most significant. The hidden curriculum of education is based on long-term gratification. Many youth do not believe they are going to live past their 18th birthday, so they decide to become a drug dealer making thousands of dollars. We must convince Black male youth that there's a better chance of them becoming an engineer, computer programmer, doctor, lawyer, scholar, and teacher than becoming a drug dealer. Schools cannot do this if they can't teach Black males how to read. Schools will continue to fail if they are adamant about retaining, suspending and placing Black males in special education.

Ask students if they know one drug dealer who has sold drugs for 15, 20, 25, or 30 years and is now retired. Inform them that drug dealers do not retire. They do one of three things: use, go to jail, or die. That's the future of a drug dealer. If we don't do anything else, we must teach them that this is what happens to drug dealers. Many teachers don't want to discuss this, but it is difficult working with students who lack motivation. It is difficult to try to empower students to pursue education when they're not convinced that education is the great equalizer. They believe crack cocaine is the great equalizer. We must disprove this notion.

Before we teach Columbus, Lincoln, or Hippocrates, let's convince Black boys that crack cocaine is not the great equalizer. It is the best way to go to jail.

Why would America spend more money to incarcerate someone than they would spend to send him to college? If the objective is to balance the budget, then Head Start, preschool programs, Title 1, and Pell Grants are much more cost effective than prison. The prison recidivism rate is 85 percent. Most states are spending more than $30,000 per inmate and experiencing only 15 percent in efficacy. Have your students discuss and write why America would spend more money to incarcerate than to educate. Why are prison guards paid more than teachers? Why are more and more prisons being owned and operated by companies in the private sector? Is there an incentive for prisons to rehabilitate inmates?

Prisons are modern day plantations. There are many southern states that have mandatory farm labor for their inmates. The same land that was formerly used to plant, pick, and harvest crops by enslaved people who came to America as shipboard captives are now planted, picked, and harvested by enslaved prison inmates who are now incarcerated captives.

I encourage you to read the excellent book by Michelle Alexander, *The New Jim Crow*. Prisons have replaced plantations. The people doing the work are descendants of the people who worked the plantations, and the people who own the prisons are descended from the people who owned the plantations.

Rev. Jesse Jackson, Sr. has often said, "The best way to put prisons out of business is not to go." Have your students write a pledge promising they will not go to prison. Make sure it's a detailed pledge that discusses how they will avoid traps of fighting, suspensions, hanging out on corners, selling drugs, and joining gangs.

Writing Assignment

Ask students which is more dangerous: the street or prison?

Have students list all the people they know who are either in prison or have been to there. Have them write a letter to at least five of those people.

Ask them if they think they will go to prison and if they're afraid of prison. Describe a day in prison. Could you defend yourself against a booty raid in prison? Let them know that many inmates are raped and infected in prison and then released into society with an HIV-positive status. Have them write a paper on the schoolhouse-to-jailhouse pipeline and address this question: Are prisons the new plantations?

Let's now move to the next chapter on fatherhood.

Chapter 19: Fatherhood and Sex Culture

As we continue to investigate the world of Black male students, we'll discover that fatherhood is a major issue that affects them. Teachers, did you know that some of your fifth- through eighth-grade students may be fathers? High school teachers, there is an even higher probability that you have student fathers in your school.

Let's say you have a fifth-grader, 10 years of age, who became sexually active at the age of nine. If he was retained twice, he's now 12 years- old in your fifth-grade class. The reality is that fatherhood has started much earlier than acceptable in the Black community. For many of our boys, the challenge is not algebra, geometry, and trigonometry, biology, chemistry, and physics. It's how a 12-year-old male with no job or parenting skills raises his child.

Ask your male students what they know about the rapper Shawty Lo? How many babies has he made? Is he a positive role model for African American males? Have them discuss and write a paper about the difference between a sperm donor and a daddy. Explain how it takes about 18 seconds to become a sperm donor and a minimum of 18 years to be a daddy. Then ask them which one they'll be and why. Have them write about their vision of what it would be like to be a father. What kind of relationship will they have with the baby's mother and family? How will your students' own family members respond to the news?

Fathers in America

African American fathers in the home:	Fathers in the home:
•1920 – 90 percent	Asian – 90
•1960 – 80 percent	White – 75 percent
•present – 28 percent [26]	Hispanic – 59 percent
	African American – 28 percent

Have students write an analysis of the causes of the decline of African American fathers in the home from 1920 to the present. Ask your students why African Americans are the lowest on the totem pole of fathers of all races. Do Black males have a disdain for their children? Why don't more Black men stay with their children? Have them draw a map of their block and indicate where are the fathers.

This next area is very sensitive. Ask students to raise their hands if their father is at home. Have them write a letter to their father. If they need to, write a letter of forgiveness, or tell their fathers that they are angry with them. Give students the safety and space to write whatever is on their hearts.

Why are there more murders in the inner city than there are in the suburbs? Why is it that a White female can walk down the block in Little Italy in Baltimore at midnight and not be bothered, but a Black female might be bothered at 12:00 noon as she walks through the ghetto? Could fathers reduce crime, gangs, and other problems in the Black community?

Consequences of fatherlessness:

- Grade retention
- Special education placement
- Illiteracy
- Suspension
- Dropping out of school
- Poverty
- Teen pregnancy
- Drug addiction
- Crime
- Incarceration

If we had more fathers in the home, we could reduce, if not eliminate, most of the social ills in the Black community. Discuss and have students write about this idea.

Can you be a father without money? Can you be a father if you cannot provide for your family? Let's revisit the above list. In 1920, 90 percent of Black fathers were in the home, and they were working either on farms or in factories. In 1960, 80 percent of Black children had their fathers in the home, and Black men were working in factories. But today, only 28 percent of Black children have their fathers in the home. America's economy has moved from the farm to the factory to the computer to overseas. Are schools preparing Black males for this computer driven economy? Later when we discuss economics, we will look at this in more detail. Does America have a need for Black male labor? Do we only need Black males to populate American prisons? Could prisons function without half their population of African American males? These are the types of questions that schools need to ask their African American male students if we're going to connect with and empower them.

What else can a father provide for his children if he can't provide financially? Discuss nurturing with your boys.

Let me share the following story of two fathers. Both men worked for the same company. The plant closed and sent the jobs overseas. The first man felt that no money, then no manhood, and no need to stay with his children. He became abusive to his wife and children, and he eventually left.

Chapter 19: Fatherhood and Sex Culture

The second man went back to school. He helped his children with their homework. He cleaned the house while the wife was at work. He made dinner before they came home. He sold newspapers and drove a taxi.

The first man is now in prison doing 20 years. The second man is closer to his children and wife, has earned a degree, and is now working in the editorial department for the newspaper he once sold on the street. We must create a school culture that will produce that second type of father.

So many times when we discuss parenting, the burden seems to exclusively fall on mothers. It is as if all fathers do is make babies, like Shawty Lo. To remedy this mind-set, divide boys into small groups of five, and give a doll to each group to take care of for one week. They will feed and care for the doll just as if it were a real baby. They will write down their experiences in a journal. Activities like playing basketball and video games will have to be curtailed because the priority is to take care of the doll. The group that has the best journals and has done the best caretaking will be given a nice prize. We must teach boys how to be fathers. If we improve school culture for Black males, we can increase this abysmal figure of only 28 percent of Black youth with fathers in the home.

What concerns me more is that there is no anguish, embarrassment, shame, guilt, urgency, or passion among young Black males to correct the problem. If anything, the Shawty Lo's are receiving more and more accolades. There was even talk about Shawty Lo having a TV reality show called *All My Babies' Mamas*. Had it not been for the outcry of the Black community, that show might have aired. We don't need any more males bragging in the locker room, barber shop, and on the corners about how many babies they have made. We must teach boys that the emphasis should be on quality parenting. It is not the number of children that's important, it's the quality of the relationship a man has with his children.

If anything, suggest the following numbers to your boys:

- 28 – Don't get married until 28 or until you feel that you have strong self-esteem.
- 30 – Wait at least two years after marriage to have children. Get to know your wife. Discuss child rearing techniques.
- 2 – Only bring into the world the number of children you can take care of. The experts recommend two.
- 4 – Spread each child four years apart. That way, each child will receive enough lap time and nurturing before the next child arrives. Also, your children should never be in college at the same time.

The reality of what's going on in the Black community is reflected in the following numbers:

- 0 – Black males are not getting married.
- 16 – Black males are having babies at 16 years of age or younger
- 9 – Some Black males have...
  - 9 children
  - with 9 mothers
  - every 9 months.

We're not going to build a strong community with the numbers 0, 16, 9 and 9. You build a strong community with the numbers 28, 30, 2, and 4.

Sexuality

Forty-one percent of Black male teenagers have an STD.[27] Have your students list the top five STDs. Have them write a paper on each one.

African Americans are only 13 percent of the national population but as of 2010, 51 percent of the males in America with AIDS are African American.[28] Why is the number so high? Why are so many Black males possessing either an STD or an HIV–positive diagnosis?

Teach your boys the following mantra: *You do not have sex with a person. You have a sex with their history.*

If your students think history is boring, they may feel differently when they begin to think about the health implications of their sexual history. Every person your mate slept with, you slept with, and this could affect your health. Many youth tell me that they're virgins, yet they have an STD. When I ask them to please explain how they can be a virgin with an STD, they say something like, "But I only had oral sex." Many Black males think that oral sex is not sex. Have your male students write a paper titled, "Oral Sex Can Kill You."

Writing Assignment

Earlier we discussed how many of our boys are viewing pornography on the Internet. Discuss pornography with your male students. Have they observed pornography on the Internet? What are five popular websites? Have them write about what they have seen on those websites. Ask them if they think their view of sexuality has been affected by what they have seen.

Ask them to describe a train. Have they ever participated in a train? Were they compelled to do it because of peer pressure or a gang initiation? How would they feel if their peer group was running a train on their mother, sister, or cousin?

Ask your male students if they see Black females as queens or b–s? How you see her, more than anything else, determines how you think of her and reflects your values. Have students write a paper titled, "Are Females Queens or B–s?"

Let's now discuss the elephant in the room—racism.

Chapter 20: Racism Culture

I recently read an article about a school district that was teaching students about racial topics, including the 2012 movie *Django Unchained*. A White parent complained and felt that the discussions on race divided the students and made White children feel guilty about what happened to Black people historically. In my own work with schools, I've seen where a teacher or administrator will take a leadership role in attempting to have the conversation, but all it takes is one parent who disagrees. One parent who is an atheist can have all discussion about the Bible shut down. One racist parent can stop all thoughtful discussion about racism in the classroom. Most schools would rather be under the radar about this topic, and they usually give in to parental pressure.

Racism is the elephant in the room that most people do not want to talk about. A recent poll showed 74% of African Americans felt racism is still a major problem in America. In contrast, only 19% of Whites felt the same. Until White teachers understand and appreciate the Black experience and acknowledge racism it will be difficult to change the culture. It's even more difficult for an African American author and speaker to discuss racism with a large White teaching staff. Unfortunately, some White educators are in a state of denial.

I once gave a presentation to a school district that was 60 percent Black, 20 percent Hispanic, and 20 percent White. When I began to discuss race, a teacher politely raised her hand and said, "I am not racist, and I don't see color. I see children as children." The predominately White staff was in full agreement. They said I was discussing an issue that no longer exists. Now that we've elected a Black man as president, many people believe the country is no longer racist. Later we will look at racism from the Black male student's perspective. One of their favorite rappers, The Game, says, "F— Jesse Jackson and Al Sharpton, because it's not about racism."

I said, "After the workshop, I would like to visit your classroom because the décor of your classroom and the selection of your books and every other component in your room will let me know what you really think of these children." Remember, the school district was 60 percent Black, 20 percent Hispanic, and 20 percent White. So I'm expecting to see those same demographics reflected in her classroom. I expected to see a good percentage of Black posters on the wall and Black books in the library. What I saw was an all-White bulletin board, and almost 90 percent of the books were about White children and White culture. Remember, the teacher said she didn't see color. In my opinion, she saw it better than anyone.

I find it helpful to understand racist behavior in the context of the following four stages:

- Stage 1: Denial.
- Stage 2: Admit that race and culture are factors.
- Stage 3: Understand race and culture. Read about culture and try to understand what's going on.
- Stage 4: Appreciate the culture of others.

What stage are you in? Denial, admission, understanding, or appreciation? Now, closely tied to racism is classism. In my book, *Black Students, Middle-Class Teachers,* I state that in many cases, the superintendant is African American. The principal is African American. The administrative team is African American, and more than 50 percent of the staff is African American. But this does not mean that the Black students are liked. Some of the schools with the most special education and remedial reading placements, suspensions, dropouts, and retention rates are governed by African American superintendants, principals, and a predominately African American staff.

For some schools, it's about race. For other schools, it's classism. Is there a culture of racism in your school? Is there a culture of classism in your school? Have staff members in your school ever uttered the following statements:

- *Those* children.
- What do you expect?
- Just look at their neighborhood.
- Have you ever met the father?
- Have you ever met the mother?
- He'll probably be in prison or dead by 25.
- You can't save all of them.
- I will teach those who want to learn.

These are just some of the statements that are used in at-risk schools. If you look at them specifically, none of the statements by themselves connote racism. It's all part of the hidden Eurocentric curriculum and culture that exist in schools. And here is my acid test: do you see your students the same way you see your biological children? Do you see a Black boy in your school as your son? Some White and Black teachers both have a disdain for Black children.

Let's go further. Your school has a culture of racism or classism if the expectations of your teachers are low because of the race or income of the students. There is a culture of racism or classism if tracking is paramount in your building. To the outside world, your school may appear integrated—50 percent White, 50 percent Black—but if your advanced classes are predominately White, and your regular, remedial, and special education classes are Black and/or Latino, there is a culture of racism or classism at your school.

If African Americans and Whites are committing the same infractions, but only African Americans are being suspended, there's a culture of racism or classism in your school.

If a significantly disproportionate number of African American children are being placed in special education and are given a watered-down curriculum, there's a culture of racism or classism at your school.

If the décor—the posters and art on the walls—does not reflect the population of the students, there's a culture of racism or classism at your school.

Are you still teaching that Columbus discovered America and that Abraham Lincoln freed the slaves? Do your students know that Egypt is in Africa, not the Middle East? Did you forget to tell Black students that their ancestors developed the first civilization and the laws of math and science and built the pyramids? Do they know that the father of medicine was not Hippocrates but Imhotep? If not, there's a culture of racism or classism at your school.

Do you provide left brain lesson plans to right brain learners? All the research shows that a significant percentage of African American students, and even more African American males, are tactile and kinesthetic learners.[29] Yet in spite of the research, these schools continue to give left brain/textbook/ lectures/ videos/work sheet lesson plans to tactile and kinesthetic learners. That is a clear illustration of racism and classism.

Wade Boykin's research about cooperative learning clearly shows that African American children perform better in a cooperative learning setting. White children respond better in individualistic settings. For educators to continue to teach individualism and competition to children who perform far better in cooperative learning groups is another illustration of racism and classism.

There's a culture of racism in your school if administrators refuse to disaggregate student scores. You can't solve a problem if you don't know exactly where the problem is. The abysmal scores of Black and Hispanic students are being covered up.

Let's say half your students are Black and half are White, and the aggregated average test score is at the 60 percentile. Now let's break it down by race, and the scores are highly revealing. Black students are actually at the 40 percentile, and White students are at the 80 percentile. The 60 percent average tells you nothing about the tremendous disparity in grades by race, and this is something we need to know if we're going to help Black students. Not only are some school districts unwilling to disaggregate the scores based on race because race is the word we don't want to discuss, but they refuse to provide solutions to help the population that needs the resources the most.

Often, when I'm brought in by school districts because of their underperforming Black students, they are unwilling to tell me how acute is the problem. More importantly, they usually don't want me to speak to just Black students or just Black boys or give a workshop on what to do with this specific population. If you know your African American students are scoring at the 40 percentile, and your African American male students could be scoring as low as the 20 percentile, then when are we going to open up and be honest about what's going on? The only way to know what we're dealing with is to disaggregate the test scores. Once we know what's going on, then we can design a program. The refusal to disaggregate the scores so that we can provide solutions to help Black males is a clear illustration of a school and school district in denial and tainted by racism and classism.

If your school refuses to make an effort to improve their staffing demographics, there's a culture of racism or classism at your school. In addition, if your school has no recruitment strategy in place to increase the number of African American staff members, especially males, this is an illustration of a racist culture. Often, administrators will say they don't know where to find qualified Black teachers. If a school is serious about increasing the number of African American staff members, I strongly encourage them to appoint an African American staff member or steering committee with that responsibility. Reach out to the Black church, the National Association of Black School Educators, and the 106 Black colleges. Attend the conventions of Black fraternities and sororities. Interact with the group Call Me MISTER, which is an excellent organization designed to increase the number of African American males in the teaching corps by providing them with scholarships. Hire a Black employment search firm. Schools that have taken advantage of these resources have increased their pool of African American candidates.

Post-Traumatic Slavery Disorder

Believe it or not, I'm not trying to indict schools. The purpose of this chapter is to expose how African American male students are greatly affected by racism. It could be the number one factor affecting their destination in life, but unfortunately schools have not taught them how to recognize and successfully respond to racism. If anything, when the rapper The Game said, "F— Jesse Jackson and Al Sharpton because it's not about race," it shows how apolitical and ahistorical many Black males are and how little they understand racism in society.

There is a spirit of self-hatred and Post-Traumatic Slavery Disorder in many of our students. Your Black male students are suffering from Post-Traumatic Slavery Disorder if they believe that:

- Good hair is long and straight.
- Pretty eyes are anything but dark brown.
- The lighter you are, the prettier you are.

I encourage teachers to take another look at *106 & Park* on BET. Count the times when you see a dark–skinned, fully dressed female with short hair on a music video. It is no accident why our children, both male and female, feel the way they do.

Students are suffering from Post-Traumatic Slavery Disorder if they think that being smart is acting White, they are better in sports than science, music than math, rap than reading, if they believe they have a greater chance of making the basketball team when 200 people are trying out for 12 slots versus making the debate team or science fair team where few, if any, people try out.

You are suffering from Post-Traumatic Slavery Disorder when you have little respect for people who look like you, are willing to fight people who look like you, and are willing to curse people who look like you with the "N" or "b–" word.

A good education should prepare you to return to your neighborhood and live a better life. Racism negatively affects African American males, and we need schools and lesson plans that will boldly address this issue. We must teach Black boys how to recognize and respond to racism.

Writing Assignment

I encourage every Black male in your school to read a book about Jackie Robinson, Paul Robeson, Marcus Garvey, Frederick Douglass, Muhammad Ali, Nelson Mandela, Malcolm X, Martin Luther King, Steven Biko, Booker T. Washington, W.E.B. Du Bois, and Barack Obama. Have them write a report about how these men were affected by racism and their responses.

Discuss and have your boys write a paper on the following statements:

1. If Blacks were inferior, why was there a need to discriminate?
2. Until you understand White supremacy, everything else will confuse you.
3. The Jewish motto is "Never forget."
4. Culture can overcome racism.
5. Are you going to play the race card of excuses, or are you going to play Rule 110?

After all is said and done about racism and Post-Traumatic Slavery Disorder, can you now begin to see ways to improve your school culture for Black boys? Do you see forms of racism in your school? Can you and your colleagues begin to see Black boys as your sons? Can your lesson plans change the communication among African Americans such that they no longer call their male peers the "N" word and females "b–"? Ultimately, are we empowering African American males? Are we producing African American males who have the spirit, vigor, fight, and fortitude of Jackie Robinson, Paul Robeson, Frederick Douglass, Marcus Garvey, Muhammad Ali, Nelson Mandela, Malcolm X, Martin Luther King, Steven Biko, Booker T. Washington, W.E.B. Du Bois, and Barack Obama to understand and overcome racism?

Let's now discuss the impact capitalism has on Black males.

Chapter 21: Economics Culture

It's very difficult living in the richest country in the world as a poor person. In Black America, more than one-third of African Americans live below the poverty line. More than 38 percent of Black children live below the poverty line. Nearly 50 percent of African American households headed by a single mother live in poverty.[30]

Being poor affects all aspects of your life—whether you'll be able to eat, and if you do eat, the quality of the food. It affects your health and your ability to receive proper medical care. It affects your housing, whether you'll be homeless or moving from one apartment or house to another. It affects whether your father will stay home with you if he can't provide. If you live in a poor neighborhood, there's a good chance it won't be safe. The first concern of low-income parents is economic survival, not helping children with their homework. When you're so overwhelmed by poverty, it affects your conversation at home. It creates a spirit of hopelessness. It affects your desire to attend a PTA meeting. You think about it all the time.

How do we help Black males reconcile living so poorly in the richest country in the world where one percent of the population owns 50 percent of the wealth, and 10 percent of the population owns 90 percent of the wealth? Money is the number one priority for Black males. It is what they think about more than anything else. As many lessons as possible, but especially math should use money. We are not going to positively change the culture for Black males until we teach them how to get out of poverty and acquire income and wealth.

The Black community is not monolithic. In some schools, African American students may be only five percent of the population, and in other schools, they are 100 percent of the population. The same thing applies to economics. Not all African Americans live below the poverty line. If more than one-third of African American adults and nearly 50 percent of Black households headed by a single mother live in poverty, this means that almost two-thirds of African American adults and children do not live below the poverty line. According to data gathered by the U.S. Bureau of Labor Statistics, nearly 48 percent of African Americans earn more than $35,000 per year; almost 11 percent earn more than $200,000 per year.[31]

You could divide the Black community into three groups: upper middle class, working class, and lower class. We live in a capitalistic country where money is the means of exchange, so why are we not teaching African American males the principles of capitalism? I encourage you to read my book, *An African Centered Response to Ruby Payne's Poverty Theory*. It is amazing to me how so many teachers believe in the low-income theory, which says that as income declines, so do test scores. Why would declining income encourage you to lower your expectations? If anything, believing in the cultural and poverty deficit model should evoke *more* from you. Children in these circumstances would need *higher* expectations. They would need *more* time on task in order to overcome poverty.

If you believe that poverty is a significant factor affecting academic achievement, then why don't we teach African American males how to overcome poverty? It is difficult for Black boys to watch *106 & Park* and see rappers splitting verbs and saggin' all the way to the bank, living, apparently, in mansions and being driven in limousines, while viewers are living in a neighborhood of squalor. We must help Black boys reconcile living not only in the richest country in the world, but the country that has the greatest disparity and distribution of wealth. America is clearly a country of haves and have nots. Schools mirror capitalism with tracking. How can we in good conscience have the advanced students on one floor and the remedial students on another?

Ask your students about the various forms of acquiring wealth in America. After they give you their list, provide yours:

- Inheritance
- Entrepreneurship
- Stock market
- Real estate
- Sports
- Entertainment
- Crime
- The lottery

Let's say that wealth is more than $10 million. Discuss the different ways they think Blacks and Whites earn wealth. Ask them to list all the African Americans they know who have acquired wealth in each of the above areas.

Have them research and write a paper on Robert Johnson, John Johnson, Reginald Lewis and Magic Johnson. Have them read *Black Enterprise* magazine. Have them find and tell the story of the magazine's founder Earl G. Graves, Sr.

Since we live in a capitalistic country, we must teach Black boys capitalism. We must teach them about entrepreneurship, the stock market, and real estate. We must convince Black boys that they have a greater chance at earning $10 million or more in those areas than sports, entertainment, crime, or the lottery. Unfortunately, many African Americans believe their chances of becoming rich are greater in the last four forms of acquiring wealth than the first four.

Entrepreneurship

I encourage you to use the curriculum developed by the National Foundation for Teaching Entrepreneurship. I'm on the council of their board. They have done an excellent job of providing resource materials to help students become entrepreneurs. The founder, Steve Mariotti, was a former schoolteacher in New York. He was frustrated that his boys were doing so poorly, yet he knew they understood money so well. When he turned every math problem into a money problem, students became scholars. This resonated with Steve, and it inspired him to create the organization.

We must teach Black boys how to develop a business plan. We must teach them the components of business: production, marketing, and accounting. Remember, 20- 25 boys, five groups of five, three/four years at a time. Let's create a competition among the groups of five. Each group is to develop a business plan. The group that has the best plan will receive a cash prize hopefully of a minimum of $10,000. You can raise funds for the award by partnering with your local churches and businesses in your community. We can improve school culture for Black males if they can start and profit from businesses they create in school.

We can motivate Black boys academically and reduce their desire to drop out when they see the financial success that comes from creating an award-winning business plan. Ideally, the award will be used to implement their winning plan.

Have your students create a map of their neighborhood. On the map, have them indicate the businesses in their neighborhood. Put an "A" if it is an African American-owned business, and put an "F" if it is a foreign-owned business. Then discuss and write about who owns the businesses in the boys' neighborhood. Why do foreigners seem to do so well in African American communities?

Discuss the products and services African American consumers purchase. What must we do to increase the number of Black businesses in their neighborhoods?

What do Magic Johnson, Steve Jobs, Mark Zuckerberg, Michael Dell, Bill Gates and Mark Cuban all have/had in common? They are/were all billionaires without a college degree. In the book Rich Dad, Poor Dad, the poor dad had the degree and the rich dad either was an entrepreneur, owned stocks and or real estate.

Stock Market

Earlier, we discussed the obsession with designer gym shoes. First, let's connect gym shoes to the stock market. Have your boys research the stock prices of the different gym shoe companies. Now with play money, or real money if you can, "invest" $300 in one or more of the stocks. Throughout the year, monitor the performance of the stocks. Every first of the month, let's observe the growth of the stock and compare that to the actual shoe. Which one will appreciate over the course of the year?

Beyond Nike and the gym shoe, teach boys the principle of the stock market, which is Rule 72:

$$72 \div \text{rate of return} = \text{number of years your money will double}$$

For example, if you have $10,000 and you keep it in an interest-bearing checking account, money market account, a shoe box, or under your mattress, you will earn between 0 and 2 percent return. If you earn 2 percent in a money market or checking account, then 72 divided by 2 means it will take 36 years for your $10,000 to double and become $20,000.

However, if you invest that $10,000 in the stock market, where the average rate of return has been 12 percent, your investment will grow exponentially. Divide 72 by 12, and you will find that it will take six years for your $10,000 to double. Of course, it's important to discuss the reason for the difference in the rates of return between the stock market, bank accounts, shoe boxes, and mattresses, especially regarding the various risks involved.

Give each of your groups of five boys $10,000 of play money at the beginning of the school year. Have them invest their money in the stock market. As the bank, you will monitor their progress each month. At the end of the school year, the team that had the greatest return on their investment will receive a monetary award.

We must teach Black boys capitalism. We must teach them how to overcome poverty. There are other ways to overcome poverty than the NBA, NFL, becoming a rapper, a drug dealer, or playing the lottery. If our boys can understand capitalism, they will be able to provide an inheritance for their children. Then they will be able to participate in the four streams of income—inheritance, entrepreneurship, the stock market, and real estate—that the 1 percent and 10 percent of the country, which does include some African Americans, use to drive their wealth.

Chapter 21: Economics Culture

Real Estate

Have your boys create a map of their neighborhood. If possible, find out on a particular block how many houses or apartment buildings are owned by African Americans. Indicate on the map if there are any houses and vacant lots that are for sale or on the auction block.

Your boys need to know that gangs are fighting over turf (land, property) they do not own. Talk to them about how much it would cost to buy a house in foreclosure, rehab it, and flip (resell) the property. Can you imagine the impact, if we had mentors who would work with Black boys after school to rehab some of these buildings and when the properties sell, the boys would enjoy some of the profit? Let me share this horror story. I was consulting in this school. One of the least effective teachers not only was the union representative, but conducted real estate business during the school day. He was a slum landlord. He actually owned many of the properties where his students reside. The least he could have done was taught his students the principles of real estate.

A tremendously lucrative segment of real estate worth billions of dollars just in the U.S. alone is the commercial real estate industry. Commercial real estate is comprised of industrial, office, and retail properties—for example, malls, skyscrapers, restaurants, clothing stores, clinics, banks, hotels, warehouses, grocery stores, and office buildings. What many people do not know is that fortunes have been made in commercial real estate by providing services to building owners. Have students brainstorm some of these services. Listed below are just a few:

- Security and reception services
- Facilities management (janitorial, energy management, elevator repairs, parking lot and grounds maintenance, landscaping, etc.)
- Cafeteria management and food service
- Transport and shipping (delivery of goods via trucks, vans and other vehicles)
- Lease administration (renting)
- Brokerage (buying and selling)
- Architecture, interior design, and construction
- Capital markets (raising money to buy buildings)
- Valuation and appraisals (determining the value of a building)

Unfortunately, African Americans have made few inroads into the commercial real estate industry due to racism. Our boys need to realize that just because African Americans have been discriminated against does not mean that they cannot tear the walls down, so to speak. Magic Johnson not only invests in residential real estate, he invests in office and retail spaces. Which other famous African Americans own commercial real estate?

Have your students indicate the clothing stores, hair salons, cell phone stores, restaurants, car repair shops, car dealerships, office buildings, warehouses, and strip malls on the neighborhood maps they have drawn. Then have them note which properties are Black-owned, White-owned, and foreign-owned.

Black Enterprise holds an annual conference for junior entrepreneurs. It would be fantastic if these ideas germinated so well in your school that you were able to send groups of African American males to this national conference. If you prepared them properly, they might even win the national prize from Black Enterprise.

If you don't want to do the above, we can continue to believe Ruby Payne and all the pundits who want to make poverty the culprit and use it as an excuse for lowering expectations. Or you can raise your expectations, require more time on task, and teach boys about capitalism and how to overcome poverty. The best way to teach Black boys how to overcome poverty is to teach them entrepreneurship, the stock market, and real estate.

Writing Assignment

Have students research and write about the following:
What is a credit score?
What is a budget?
What percent is taken from your check for taxes?
What is Social Security?

Math Assignment

How long will it take to pay $1,000 in credit card debt at 18 percent interest if you only make the minimum payments?

In 10 years, how much would you have if you contributed $25 per week to a mutual fund that had a 12 percent return?

How much would you lose if you bought $25 per week in lottery tickets for one year—and didn't win? Ten years? Which zip codes in the city spend the most on the lottery?

If we do not teach Black males entrepreneurship, investing, and real estate, they will dependent on someone to employ them. Listed below are the employment statistics for Black males.

Percentage of Black working-age (16-64) males employed in 40 selected cities:[32]

Chapter 21: Economics Culture

1) Detroit 43.0%
2) Buffalo 43.9%
3) Milwaukee 44.7%
4) Cleveland 47.7%
5) Chicago 48.3%
6) St. Louis 51.3%
7) Philadelphia 51.7%
8) Phoenix 52.0%
9) Indianapolis 52.6%
10) Cincinnati 52.6%
11) Richmond 52.7%
12) Memphis 53.2%
13) Pittsburgh 53.3%
14) Hartford 53.3%
15) San Francisco 53.3%
16) Miami 53.4%
17) New Orleans 53.5%
18) Oakland 53.8%
19) Omaha 53.8%
20) Las Vegas 54.2%
21) Birmingham 54.3%
22) Newark 54.5%
23) Columbus (Ohio) 54.7%
24) Jacksonville 54.8%
25) Los Angeles 54.8%
26) Kansas City 55.1%
27) Seattle 56.3%
28) Charlotte 56.5%
29) San Diego 57.1%
30) Portland (Oregon) 57.4%
31) New York 57.4%
32) Baltimore 57.5%
33) Houston 58.3%
34) Nashville 58.4%
35) Denver 58.8%
36) Atlanta 59.0%
37) Minneapolis 59.3%
38) Boston 59.7%
39) Dallas 61.0%
40) Washington, DC 66.6%

Writing Assignment

What is your school doing to better prepare Black males for employment? Have your boys discuss and write about these figures.

We will now discuss how to develop your male students to be leaders.

Chapter 22: Leadership Culture

Does your school produce Black male leaders?

Does your culture, curriculum, pedagogy develop Black boys to their fullest potential?

Is your school equipped and designed to produce men like President Barack Obama, pediatric neurosurgeon Ben Carson, and entrepreneur Robert Johnson?

Too many of our schools have produced dropouts and illiterates. Many schools have created a military-style culture. They feel the best way to teach a Black male is to break him down. There is nothing worse than to see a Black boy whose spirit has been broken. In this chapter, we will explore how to develop a boy's spirit like an eagle. We want to develop leaders. We want to develop Black males who not only excel academically, but have the personality traits of a leader.

Manhood/Masculinity

Let's look at and define manhood by using a pyramid. Spiritual will be at the top, mental and physical at the bottom.

As this pyramid indicates, manhood is a perfect balance between mental, physical, and spiritual. Unfortunately, Black males tend to emphasize the physical to the detriment of their mental and spiritual development. In addition to dunking a basketball, lifting 200 pounds, and running 100 meters in under 11 seconds, our job is to help them become honor roll students. We want them to be comfortable in honors, gifted & talented, and AP classes. We also want Black males to be spiritually sound.

Ask your boys to identify the strongest within them: mental, physical, or spiritual. Have them write about their selection and give reasons for it.

What is the difference between a male, a boy, and a man? First, you are born male. It's your birthright, and you have no responsibilities. Second are boys, they love to play. Young boys play with toys. Older boys, who can be 30 years of age and older, play with women and children. The third category is a man. A man does more than play. A man takes responsibility for his actions and develops himself to his fullest potential. We want a school culture that develops males into men.

We want to help boys understand that they must break the cord from their mothers. Ask your males if they're "mama's boys." Do their mothers defend them even when they are wrong? Do their mothers have double standards for their sons and daughters? Do they make their daughters come in early, but not their sons? Do they make their daughters do chores, but not their sons? Do they make their daughters do homework, but not their sons? Do they make their daughters go to church, but not their sons? Are their sisters more responsible than they are? How long will you stay in your mother's house? We want to develop males into men who can break the cord from their mothers.

Leadership Training

Leaders are made, and it is our job to help instill in our boys the values, skills, strengths, and more that they will need to become leaders of their communities. The following are some of the ways we can train boys to become responsible leaders.

Community Service Projects. There's such a disconnection between what goes on in schools and the neighborhood. You can often tell what people think of their community by the orderliness and cleanliness that exist. How long does it take for a broken window to be repaired? There's too much litter in the Black community. There's too much graffiti in the Black community. There's too much noise in the Black community. There are too many houses that are boarded up, too many vacant lots overtaken by weeds and garbage. One of the best ways to help students appreciate their education is when their education improves the quality of life in their neighborhood. Schools must begin to use their resources to improve the décor and beauty of the neighborhood.

I'm aware that we live in a world of the common core curriculum and high stakes testing. However, if we could allocate just one hour a week for a community project, then the culture of the school will begin to change the neighborhood.

When African American males get involved in removing litter from the streets and parks, painting over graffiti, and removing weeds from vacant lots, they will respond differently when they see their friends littering and doing negative things to deface the community. This has a much more long-term effect than we think on the quality of life in the neighborhood. Now we are creating leaders.

After-School Program. There must be a dedicated time scheduled for leadership training, and I suggest an after-school program. I recommend having a mandatory after-school program that would run a minimum of three hours after school. All the research shows that young people are at the highest risk of being involved in negative activities the first three hours after school. This is particularly significant for African American males.

Note the word *mandatory*. Ideally, all boys would have to participate in the after-school program. If your school's resources or facility is inadequate or you cannot enforce a mandatory program, make the program optional for as many boys as your resources can accommodate. If there's a funding challenge, hopefully local churches, businesses,

Chapter 22: Leadership Culture

colleges, the park district, and community organizations can provide the resources that are needed.

Your after-school program should consist of leadership development, academics, community service, and recreation—all *supervised.* This program is really more labor-intensive than capital-intensive. It requires simply having people who would be willing to provide direction and supervision during these three hours. You already have the resources in your building, including a library, computer lab, gymnasium, a music room, and an art room.

I do not recommend that boys play basketball the entire three hours of the program. Granted, it would keep them off the street and therefore not get involved with crime, but let's keep our expectations high for this program. Let's focus on leadership development. Sometimes we have to use what they value most (basketball) as a carrot to motivate them to attend, especially if the program is optional.

Chess. The first objective in the after-school program is that all the boys learn the game of chess. There's excellent research on the benefits of chess.[33]

1. Chess improves attention span. If we can increase boys' attention span, we can reduce their placement into special education.
2. Chess develops critical thinking skills, which are absolutely necessary for leadership development and matriculation through college.
3. Chess improves GPA and test scores. That's why chess tops my list of activities for the after-school program.

Martial Arts. A leader must learn how to channel his fighting instinct. We know that our boys like physical activities. Unfortunately, many like to fight. We want to provide supervised physical activities, and we want to teach them self-discipline and self-defense. Recently in the media, more and more stories about school bullying have made headlines. One of the best ways to stop a bully is with a black belt.

Rites of Passage. We need to teach boys what it means to be a leader and a man. Unfortunately, their culture defines manhood based on how many girlfriends they have, how many babies they've made, whether they smoke or drink, how many crimes they've committed, whether they've shot or killed someone, and whether they've gone to prison. We need to define for boys what it means to be a man. In addition, this leadership training and rites of passage would also teach anger management.

If there's not enough time during the school day for leadership classes, the after school program provides the perfect block of time for rites of passage activities.

When our boys go through rites of passage, just like pledging in a fraternity, there's a big ceremony with lots of glory, honor, and accolades.

The larger community is invited, and our boys are honored for successfully completing their leadership training and rites of passage.

Anger Management. I strongly encourage every school to implement Positive Behavioral Interventions and Supports (PBIS). This excellent program helps boys manage their anger, own up to their mistakes, accept feedback, and learn how to apologize. Boys learn respect for authority and home training. Research has found that PBIS has reduced school suspensions by almost 66 percent.[34] This is a proactive program that helps boys to understand how their choices lead to certain consequences.

Exercises for Leadership Development
Time exercise. One of the strongest traits of a leader is his ability to manage time. Whether you are Black or White, male or female, everyone starts out with 24 hours. The game of life is designed around how well you use your 24 hours to develop your talents. Consider the lives of Tupac, Martin Luther King, and Malcolm X.

Tupac only lived to be 26 years old, but even after his death, seven CDs were released. He was very prolific and productive in his young life. Martin Luther King and Malcolm X only lived to be 39 years old. Yet, in the short amount of time they were alive, they achieved so much.

Successful people say that the first hour of the day is the most important. If you want to be great, you must maximize that first hour. Have your boys write in their journal how they usually spend the first hour of the day. Have them develop a project schedule describing what they will do and when they will do it. How could they better maximize their time?

African American males spend 38 hours per week watching television, 21 hours per week playing video games, and endless hours listening to gangsta rap and playing basketball. To help our boys become great leaders, we must teach them how to manage their time more efficiently.

Friends exercise. Great leaders select their friends with care. Have your boys write the names of their three closest friends. Next to their friends' names, have your boys write what they think their friends' GPA is and what they think they'll be doing at 30 years of age. There's an old saying: "The fruit does not fall very far from the tree." If you want to understand yourself better, all you have to do is observe your selection of friends. Your friends reflect your values, aspirations, and makeup.

There is a distinction between a friend and an associate. A friend would never lie on you, discourage you, or set you up. Have your boys write down the names of their true friends and associates.

Attitude exercise. Life is 10 percent what happens to you and 90 percent how you respond to life events. Many of our boys have a chip on their shoulders. They have a bad attitude. They blame other people for

146

their circumstances. They blame their parents, neighborhood, and teachers. We want to develop males who will take responsibility for their success. We want boys to have a positive attitude. We want to teach boys that the glass is half-full and not half-empty.

Have your boys read and write about the life of Magic Johnson. He was at the height of his career in the NBA as an All-Star. Unfortunately, he became HIV-positive. That was the 10 percent that happened to him. He could have given up and died, but because Magic Johnson has a positive, optimistic attitude (just look at his smile), he has been able to turn a negative into a positive. He moved from being a top professional in the NBA to becoming a multimillion-dollar entrepreneur. Tell your boys Magic earns more as an entrepreneur than a basketball player. That would not have happened with a pessimistic, negative attitude.

Power of words exercise. Proverbs 18:21 reminds us that death and life are in the power of the tongue. Your future is in your mouth. You cannot go any further than your words. If you believe that you are better in sports than in science, you will be. If you believe you're better in music than math, then you will be. If you believe you're a better rapper than reader, then that will be the case. If you believe you have a greater chance at making the basketball team versus the science fair or debate team, you will. You will have whatever you say.

Challenge your boys and ask them if they could go one day without using profanity or saying the "N" word or "b–" word. Ask them if they could go one day without saying the word "can't" or making a negative statement. The ultimate objective is to speak positively and powerfully for the rest of their lives.

Goals exercise. Have your students read and discuss the life of President Barack Obama, who, at the young age of nine in fourth grade, had a goal to be President of the United States of America. He became exactly what he desired. I don't believe you're at risk because you're Black. I don't believe you're at risk because you're male. I don't believe you're at risk because you're poor. I believe you're at risk when you don't have goals.

Research shows that boys will resist joining gangs and making mistakes when they have something to lose. When Black boys know they have a bright future ahead of them—when they know they're going to college, when they know they're going to be an engineer, when they know they're going to become a millionaire—they'll be more cautious about making mistakes.

Have your boys develop a five-year plan. What will they be doing during the next five years? Next, have them write about what they'll be doing 10, 20, 30, and 40 years from now.

Have them write a résumé or even an autobiography. Have them write a letter to an employer, asking for a job and explaining why they would be good candidates.

Values exercise. Values are fundamental to strong leadership. We have discussed at length some of the values our boys have that are keeping them from performing to the best of their ability. Your values are a reflection of how you think and behave. Since our boys receive their values, not from parents and church, but from rappers, media, peers, and video games, we must teach them about values that are life-affirming and will lead to success in school and life.

The goal of the values exercise is to help students identify their strengths and challenges, which is critical in leadership development. Ask students if they have a strong work ethic. Are you tenacious? Are you responsible? Do you keep your word? Do you tell the truth? In this exercise, have your boys rate themselves on a scale from 1 to 10 around the following four values:

- Ethics
- Tenacity
- Responsibility
- Truth

Discuss their ratings and show them how they apply to school and their relationships with friends, family, and teachers. Ask them have they ever cheated on a test? Have a discussion with them about the Atlanta cheating scandal. Earlier, in the school culture chapter, I mentioned the homeless man who found a backpack filled with $4000 and computer equipment. Ask yourself and your students, if that had been you in the same circumstance, what would you do?

Choices and consequences exercise. Students have 10 seconds to make a decision that could cost them their lives.

CHOICE	CONSEQUENCES
Drop off a drug package.	Receive $500 or go to jail.
Get in a car with a gang member or drug dealer.	Have a lot of fun or go to jail.
Run a train on a female.	Have a lot of fun, get an STD or go to jail.
Someone hits you, so you hit him back.	Retaliation or suspension.

Do not study; watch television, and play video games.	Have fun or receive a low GPA; no scholarship.
Slack off during team practice.	Be less fit or do not play. Coach suspends you.
Violate curfew.	Have a lot of fun or go to jail.
Drive a car without a license and insurance.	Have a lot of fun or have an accident or injure someone. Jail or prison.
Get high off beer, wine, marijuana, or some other drug.	Have a lot of fun or vomit and become ill.
Buy a pair of Air Jordan gym shoes.	Everyone is impressed with the shoes or someone kills you for the shoes.

We must teach our boys the power of choices and consequences. Try role playing these various choices with your students. Let your boys suggest choices and consequences that are not on the list. They can be something their friends are actually going through, or they can be made up. In real life, they have less than 10 seconds to make the right decision. Life is about choices, and Satan is quick to remind us of how fun they will be, but he doesn't tell us about the possible consequences of our actions. It is our job as educators, leaders, and parents to help our boys understand the full consequences of their behavior. Leaders recognize that choices have consequences and often, there isn't much time to weigh the options and consequences and discern the best choice to make. Still, leaders aim for the best choice—the one with the most ethical consequences that align with their values.

Next, have your boys participate in the following exercise about choices. Choose one:

- The finest car money can buy
- All the clothes you could ever wear
- A multimillion-dollar mansion
- Time
- 100,000 acres of land
- $10 million

Have a discussion and have them write about their choice.

Psychology of performance exercise. Success or failure can be attributed to one of the following four factors:

- Ability
- Effort
- Luck
- Nature of the task

If you earned an A on a math test, you would either attribute it to your ability ("I'm smart in math"), effort ("I studied hard"), luck ("I win a lot"), or the nature of the task ("The test was easy").

If you did poorly on the math test, you would attribute failure to a lack of ability ("I'm not good in math"), effort ("I did not study"), luck ("I was unlucky"), or nature of the task ("The test was hard").

Let's focus on ability and effort. The research shows that girls attribute their success to their effort.[35] They believe that if they study hard, they will do well in any particular endeavor. Unfortunately, many boys attribute their success to their ability. We have mentioned how large and insecure is the male ego. Boys do not want to participate in activities where they question their ability. The tragedy is that many boys give up too easily. They also make many wrong choices. Even though their skills may be lacking in a particular area, they need to know that they can still improve through study and practice.

Michael Jordan and Ray Allen would not have been exceptional basketball players if they did not practice. If those two athletes had questioned their ability, they would have never reached the pinnacle of success. Remember, Michael Jordan did not even make his freshman team in high school. He had to work hard in the summer to make his sophomore basketball team. We must help boys understand the distinction between ability and effort. Applied time on task will strengthen skills and ability in any area they choose.

In motivational theory, research shows the best way to motivate someone is to convince them of their strengths in certain areas. Teachers must encourage boys more and improve their confidence. We must refrain from having an illiterate boy read aloud or go to the board and fail publicly doing a math problem. The other component of motivational theory is providing lessons that are relevant. We can motivate Black males if we connect our lessons to sports, rap and money.

Leadership Strategies

Schools can develop Black male leaders through the following additional strategies:

- Create a school council made up of educators, parents, and students, particularly Black male students.
- Reduce negative peer pressure by having students wear a business uniform. No saggin' pants or gym shoes allowed.
- Set apart a group of boys who have successfully completed the leadership training by having them wear a different color shirt and tie. This would illustrate the successful completion of a rite of passage into leadership.
- Take the graduates of the leadership training on a field trip to Morehouse College where they can observe Black males at the collegiate level.

Writing Assignment

The following are excellent movies that you should share with your boys and are perfect for stimulating discussion and writing assignments around leadership.

Boyz n the Hood

Remember the Titans

Courageous

When We Were Kings

Ali

Malcolm X

Eyes on the Prize

Cry Freedom

Gifted Hands

The Great Debaters

Roots

Mandela

The Second Chance

Antwone Fisher

Coach Carter

Facing the Giants

Pursuit of Happyness

Django Unchained

Snitch

In the next chapter we will discuss single-gender culture.

Chapter 23: Single-Gender Culture

Throughout this book, I have asked have designed a female classroom for male students? For some reason, schools have become so comfortable designing female classrooms that many of us aren't even aware that this is diabolical to the interests of male students.

For example, can you imagine a school with cooperative learning groups, an 83 percent male teaching staff, homework only given once a week, exercise scheduled every hour on the hour PE and recess daily, library books mostly on sports, hip hop, animals, science fiction, and technology, classroom temperature at 69 degrees, no chairs in the classroom, tables replaced desks, most classes taught outside, and aggression was rewarded?

Clearly, most schools do not have male classrooms or strategies in place. The traditional classroom has been designed to appeal to female teachers and students. We expect boys to successfully navigate the female classroom, and if they can't or won't, they are retained, placed in remedial reading and special education, suspended, or they drop out. Remember, even White males are placed in special education, remedial reading and retained more than White females.

I have been an advocate of single-gender classrooms and schools since 1985. I gave a keynote speech at the National Association of Black School Educators that year in Portland, Oregon. I had just released my best seller, *Countering the Conspiracy to Destroy Black Boys*. I told the audience that for some reason, we don't have a problem with a single-gender classroom when boys are misbehaving. Single gender seems to be okay for special education classrooms, remedial reading, or retention. For some reason we seem to be hesitant about implementing single gender from a proactive standpoint.

Now that was in 1985. Almost 30 years later there is still some resistance, primarily from the ACLU. There used to be resistance from the National Organization of Women (NOW). They felt we were in violation of Title 9 legislation and that single-gender classrooms and schools would be detrimental to females. It has only been in the past decade that we have seen an increase in the number of single-gender classrooms and schools. Feminists found that when female students are in a single-gender environment, they become more confident pursuing careers in medicine, engineering, accounting, computer programming, etc.

I'm pleased that the last two U.S. Secretaries of Education have also endorsed single-gender classrooms and schools. They have made it easier for school districts and schools to implement single-gender programs (classrooms and schools).

Some of my peers remain hesitant about endorsing single-gender classrooms and schools, and I understand part of their concern. Single gender is not a panacea. Many schools and districts have implemented single gender only to find the same abysmal test scores if not worse. You can't successfully implement single gender with a CEO principal. Single gender is not effective with principals who spend more time in the office than they do walking the corridors and visiting classrooms. A single-gender program has a better chance of succeeding when the principal is committed to being the instructional leader of the school.

Single gender is less effective if the culture has not changed. If staff believes in the Ruby Payne deficit model, then single-gender programs will not correct the problems.

Single gender is less effective when Custodians, Referral Agents, and Instructors dominate the teaching staff, and they have low expectations of students. They surely will not be effective if they insist on using a Eurocentric curriculum and left brain lesson plans with right brain students. In addition, single-gender classrooms and schools really need a committed cadre of Black male teachers.

Single gender will be less effective if the emphasis is on "I" and competition rather than "we" and cooperation. Throughout this book, we have attempted to document the significance of cooperative learning as a major tool for creating a better climate for African American males.

Schools are still into high stakes testing. If tests are being used as evaluation instruments rather than diagnostic tools, then unfortunately, single-gender classrooms and schools are not going to be less effective.

Let me now share from a quantitative perspective some of the results we have seen from single-gender classrooms and schools.

"Researchers at Stetson University in Florida completed a three-year pilot project comparing single-sex classrooms with coed classrooms at Woodward Avenue Elementary School, a nearby neighborhood public school. For example, students in the fourth grade at Woodward were assigned either to single-sex or coed classrooms. All relevant parameters were matched: the class sizes were all the same, the demographics were the same, all teachers had the same training.... On the FCAT (Florida Comprehensive Assessment Test), were the results:
- Boys in coed classes – 37 percent scored proficient.
- Girls in coed classes – 59 percent scored proficient.
- Girls in single-sex classes – 75 percent scored proficient.
- Boys in single-sex classes – 86 percent proficient."[36]

Chapter 23: Single-Gender Culture

Among the best single-gender schools for males are Eagle Academy for Young Men (New York) and Urban Prep Academies (Chicago). Tim King is the founder of Urban Prep, and David Banks is the founder of Eagle Academy. Both are good friends, and I commend them for the work they are doing with young African American males.

Eagle Academy has several campuses in the New York area, but we're going to look at the flagship campus in Brooklyn. New York City requires students to pass five Regents Exams to graduate from high school. One hundred percent of eighth-graders took three Regents Exams in June 2011. Seventy-five percent of the students at Eagle in Brooklyn passed. Twenty-six of the same class passed the Algebra I Regents Exam while in the seventh grade. When boys entered Eagle in the sixth grade, only 17 percent were reading at grade level. As of June 11, 2011, 84 percent of the same students are reading on or above grade level, received an A on the Department of Education report card, was the only school in District 23 to receive an A, and outperformed 85 percent of the schools in New York City. Eagle Academy maintained a 95 percent attendance rate.[37]

There is nothing wrong with Black students who attend schools like Eagle.

Urban Prep was founded in 2006. There flagship school is located in the poorest neighborhood in Chicago, Englewood. Only 4 percent of the school's first freshman class was reading at grade level when they entered. Four years later, the 107 graduating seniors were *all* accepted into four-year colleges. This success was repeated everyyear.[38]

Urban Prep has been wildly successful because they changed the culture for the students. They created a culture where graduating from high school was just the beginning. The objective was to be accepted into a four-year college and then graduate. On the first day of school every freshman is given a college application to complete and they visit colleges in the first semester. Remember, Urban Prep was created in a neighborhood where the high school graduation rate was only 35 percent. Less than 10 percent of that number was accepted into four-year colleges.[39] Now 100 percent of students at Urban Prep are accepted into college. This drastic increase from 10 percent to 100 percent illustrates how important culture is to students.

One of the major reasons for the success of Eagle Academy is that the principal, staff, and teachers understand how important mentoring is to boys, especially boys who lack fathers. The objective has been that every student will have a mentor. This has drastically changed the culture. At Urban Prep, close to 60 percent of their teachers are male.[40] One of the most effective ways to convince African American males that academics is masculine is for them to see scholars and educators who look like them.

Urban Prep and Eagle Academy are part of a larger network of schools called the Coalition of Schools Educating Boys of Color (COSEBOC). Visit their website (www.coseboc.org) and secure more information about the great work of the COSEBOC schools.

I'd now like to offer what I feel is the ideal male classroom.

- A single gender classroom
- A right-brain classroom
- 17 students or less
- 6 learning centers: visual-print, visual-pictures, auditory, oral, kinesthetic, tactile
- Technology center
- Famous pictures of Black/Hispanic males on the wall
- Portable tables
- No chairs
- Teacher's desk in the center of student semi-circle
- Cooperative learning groups and learning buddies
- *Best Books for Boys* in classroom and school library
- Photos of male students on the wall
- P.E. daily
- Water, juice, and fruit available for snacking
- Maximum 22-minute lectures
- 69 degrees
- Classical or jazz music in the background
- Academic competitions
- Question are encouraged
- Only open-ended questions are asked by teachers
- Two extra hours of academics and recreation
- Booker T. Washington/W.E.B. DuBois Role Model Program
- Chess and checkers
- Discipline model: unity-criticism-unity (from my book, *Developing Positive Self-Images and Discipline in Black Children*)[1]
- A maximum of 22 minutes of homework
- Homework is only one-tenth of the classroom grade
- Use money to teach various concepts
- Tests are given during the best day and time for students
- Only 20 percent of lesson plans use textbooks and ditto sheets
- Outdoor classes weather permitting
- Daily recess which can never be denied
- Weekly field trips
- Monthly community service projects
- Male mentors
- Aggression is encouraged
- Shoot a ball into a can with every correct answer

Chapter 23: Single-Gender Culture

I encourage you to consider the above classroom best practices for your coed classrooms.

I'm convinced that most schools do not know how to properly channel male energy. Black boys are often labeled "hyperactive," but what is a normal level of activity? Could it be possible that Black males are not hyperactive but have a higher energy level than White girls? There is a difference.

Why must education be confined to a chair, desk, building, and classroom? We have found that you can increase students' time on task and attention span if you allow them to have class outdoors where they can stretch and get away from a classroom's four drab walls. Something as simple as having class outdoors and providing more field trips would positively change the culture for African American males.

Some of the qualitative benefits of single-gender classrooms include:

1. Boys are more comfortable pursuing language arts, fine arts and foreign languages in a single-gender environment.
2. Boys are more willing to take risks—to read aloud, to work math problems at the board—in a single-gender environment.
3. It's okay to be smart and male in a single-gender environment. In fact, cooperative learning is even more effective in a single-gender environment.
4. There are fewer disciplinary problems. I would think reducing disciplinary problems would be a reason in itself to implement single-gender classrooms and schools. Many teachers tell me they spend almost half their day disciplining students. We could change the culture if we simply implemented single-gender classrooms and schools.
5. There is greater time on task.

In preparing teachers to work in single-gender environments, we have to be honest with them and let them know that there will be more testosterone, louder class sessions, more aggression, more movement, and they will challenge your authority. Not all teachers can handle a loud classroom with movement and aggressive students challenging their authority.

Black Male Calendar

Let's develop a school calendar based on the interests of your boys, including sports, hip hop, and hopefully, with your assistance, their culture and history. I recommend the following school calendar:

- August – sports tryouts and Marcus Garvey
- September – sports tryouts
- October – BET Hip Hop Awards
- November – High school football playoffs

- December – NCAA football/NFL ballgames and Kwanzaa
- January – Martin Luther King and NFL playoffs
- February – Black History Month and Super Bowl
- March – High school and NCAA basketball
- April – Spring break
- May – Malcolm X, NBA playoffs, graduation
- June – Graduation

I dare you to try implementing a single-gender classroom with 20/f 25 boys, for three/four years with the same Master Teacher. All I'm asking you to do is to try. We've tried everything else. It is obvious that retaining boys is not the solution. It is obvious that placing boys in special education is not the solution. It is obvious that keeping boys in remedial reading and expecting them to graduate on grade level is not working. It is obvious that suspending them for 10, 20, 30 days per year is not working. It is obvious that with a dropout rate that hovers near 50 percent, we must consider other strategies to rescue our boys.

Can you imagine, if we had a single-gender class, kindergarten through second and third through fifth with a Master Teacher? If we had a single-gender classroom sixth grade through eighth and high school with four Master Teachers, one each for language arts, math, social studies, and science? All I'm asking you to do is try.

Writing Assignment

Have your boys draw a vertical line straight down the middle of a sheet of paper. At the top of the left column, write "PROS." At the top of the right column, write "CONS." Now have students list out the pros and cons, as they see it, of single-gender classrooms and schools.

In the last chapter, we look at some additional solutions.

Chapter 24: Miscellaneous Solutions

In this chapter, I will describe several ways to improve school culture for Black males that have worked in highly progressive, highly successful schools.

Peer Mentoring

Peer pressure does not have to be negative. Peer pressure can also be positive. Peer pressure does not have to discourage academic achievement. It does not have to promote the concept that being smart is acting White or feminine. Moreover, throughout this book I have reinforced the importance of cooperative learning and that African American males perform much better in cooperative groups.

In one type of peer mentoring program, upper-grade students mentor lower-grade students for two years. Every fifth grade male would mentor a third grade male, every seventh-grade male would have the responsibility of mentoring a fifth-grade male for two years. Every 11th-grade male would mentor a ninth-grade male for two years. The benefits of this concept are that when the third –grader becomes a fifth –grader he returns the favor. The fifth-grader becomes a seventh-grader, he returns the favor. He becomes the mentor. When the ninth-grader becomes the 11th-grader, he becomes the mentor. One of the most effective ways to change school culture for African American males is by using the number one influence in their lives—their peer group—and to use that group to give them a sense of direction. One of the best programs in the country is the Minority Achievement Committee in Shaker HTS Ohio. They have provided peer mentoring since the mid 1990s. I encourage you to review their video on You Tube

Ideally, peer mentors would be given leadership training. If you lack the resources to implement a school-wide program, remember our mantra: 20-25 boys, three/ four years at a time. Simply start with fifth — grade boys who will mentor third-grade boys for two years, and expand the program as resources allow.

So often people become overwhelmed by problems in our school system. They are overwhelmed by the dropout rate of 50 percent, the large number of Black boys who are in special education or remedial reading or who have a low GPA. As a result, inertia kicks in and they don't do anything. If you could simply start with 20-25 boys, you would make a difference. Let's start there.

I also recommend that an adult male mentor be assigned to each boy. Because so many schools have so few African American male teachers, we must provide strong Black male mentors for our boys. There are many ways that this can be done. For example, Eagle Academy in New York has been so successful because each of the male students is assigned a positive male mentor. I understand that this might not be logistically possible at your school, but it does not mean that you should not try. That's why it's important to reach out to the larger community to create partnerships: one church, one school; one business, one school. These types of relationships, if properly nourished, will supply your boys with much-needed mentors.

This burden should not be borne solely by the principal. Every teacher should be able to identify one positive Black male mentor who would be willing to volunteer at the school once a week or once a month. In the excellent book *Mentor or Die,* author Kevin Hall documents that mentoring programs not only reduce the dropout rate, but they improve Black males' GPA from 1.06 to 2.8. There have been numerous studies showing the benefits of mentoring.

Baruti Kafele is the former principal of Newark Technical High School. He created the concept of "power Mondays," where the adult and younger males of the school got together and had a dialogue with one another. This helped change the culture of the school and raised test scores. He did this with the help of his male staff and invited mentors to come in on Mondays. It doesn't matter what day of the week you have it, but consider having a power day during the week. Bring all your males and mentors together and have honest discussions about what it means to be a man.

One of my most enjoyable speaking engagements was in Prince George's County, Maryland. They brought me in as the keynote speaker for a Black male convocation, but unlike most speeches where I give the speech and that's it and there's very little follow-up, the program included the presence of 200 male mentors. After my presentation, the 200 mentors met with 200 boys, and they had a discussion about my speech and other challenges facing the young people's lives.

Convocations

One of the reasons for the success of HBCUs is the weekly or monthly convocation. Have a weekly or monthly convocation at your school where you bring your boys together and discuss issues that are pertinent to them. Then follow up the convocation by having the mentors spend time with the mentees. Even though Prince George's County was fortunate to be able to provide 200 men for the 200 boys, if you have fewer mentors than boys, the main thing is that our boys are mentored.

Parallel that with the issue of counseling. In so many schools there are a thousand students, but only four counselors. So there's a 250:1 ratio of students to counselors. Our boys need direction. They need to be mentored. They need to be counseled. Mentoring is an excellent strategy to circumvent the shortage of counselors.

I appeal to the administrative team to identify churches and businesses in the community that will partner with your school. I appeal to administrators to partner with junior and four-year colleges. Our boys can take field trips to college campuses, churches, and businesses and spend time receiving direction from mentors.

Colleges can also provide tutors for your school. In fact, every student, or at least 20-25 boys at a time, should be given a tutor. Many African American males do not want to admit that they need a tutor. I've even observed at the collegiate level that young adult males will drop out of college rather than admit they need a tutor. Black males do not understand the psychology of performance. Girls understand that their success is predicated more on their effort than their ability. Boys feel just the opposite, and if their ability is not producing A's in reading or math, they begin to question their ability. We must convince Black boys of the importance of effort, and we must assist them by providing tutors. Ballplayers have coaches and trainers. President Obama has advisors.

Earlier, I mentioned that businesses can help fund the awards that will be given to the winners of the best business plan and stock market portfolio. We also need businesses to provide internships. Business mentors can help our boys role play the interviewing process. One of the best ways to change school culture for Black males is to convince them that there are people and institutions out there that want to assist them. We can reduce the dropout rate when boys have the opportunity to participate in internships after school. Too many schools are trying to change their culture without the assistance of the larger community. That is a critical mistake. If we're going to successfully change school culture, we have to partner, not only with parents, but with the larger community of churches, businesses, colleges, and community organizations.

Improve Parent-School Partnership

If we are going to change the culture, we must be humble and not arrogant with parents. We must give them respect. We must tell them, "You know your child better than I. Tell me what can I do maximize your child's academic performance? How does your child learn? What are his strengths and weaknesses? Can we work together?

Home visits. Ideally, principals should make visits to students' homes mandatory. Several school districts have mandatory home visit policies, and others simply encourage home visits. In most school districts, however, teachers are not required or encouraged to visit students' homes.

If we are going to change school culture, we must form a greater partnership between schools and homes. We used to have a village.

Teachers and parents were on the same side. Unfortunately today, parents will believe their child's story, go up to the school, and curse the teacher (and even the principal) in front of the child and even the entire classroom or school. Likewise, teachers make derogatory comments about parents in the school and sometimes in front of students. We must begin to respect one another and get to know one another better.

Monthly potluck supper. I'm not recommending that this activity be implemented school-wide. I suggest implementing a monthly potluck supper class by class. Most parents are not interested in the entire school. They tend to be interested in what's going on in their child's class. If you can create a time when parents can come together on a monthly or quarterly basis in your class with a potluck meal, I think you will see a tremendous improvement in the climate and culture of your class.

One area that parents and teachers could discuss is homework. How can a student receive a B on the mid-term exam, an A on the comprehensive final, and only receive a C for a final grade? Could it be that some teachers give more weight to homework? Could it be that the young man received a B on the mid-term and an A on the final, but because he didn't turn in more than 50 percent of his homework and because he did not participate to your satisfaction in class, you gave him a C for a final grade? You can't say that homework was necessary for him to master the information because remember, he aced your final exam.

This subject should be up for discussion at one of your potluck suppers. Why is homework assigned, and how should homework be weighted in relationship to the final grade? Do we give homework because we think it will improve the mastery of the content? Do we give homework because we want to keep children busy? Are we aware of the research that shows that if a boy has 10 challenging homework questions, he will do that in 30 minutes, but if he has 10 to 50 easy questions, it may take him several hours to complete them? For some reason boys don't like their intelligence to be insulted. They don't like being asked to do something and you both know they know the answer. They don't like their time to be wasted with time-consuming, insignificant work.

During the potluck supper, let's have an honest discussion with parents about homework—and let's have an honest discussion among ourselves as educators. Has weighted homework been detrimental to the final grade? Homework should have a 10 percent or less impact on the final grade.

A school uniform is another topic that could be discussed during a potluck supper. There are conflicting views on the efficacy of school uniforms. Many schools rave about what it has done to help students focus on academics, raise GPAs and reduce peer pressure. They feel it has reduced their clothing costs especially in the area of gym shoes. "Many schools do not allow gym shoes to eliminate the problem with those special $200 shoes." Others feel it discriminates against low-income children. They argue that you seldom observe suburban students wearing uniforms. Some feel inner city uniforms remind them of prison apparel. Ironically, in wealthy communities the students often wear a business uniform. They are being prepared to run the country. This is the uniform I am recommending. We can eliminate saggin' in school. . I am also very cognizant that the students at Urban Prep had to educate the staff that their corporate uniform could get them killed on the streets. They convinced the staff they needed to change their attire to navigate the mean streets.

Excellence for All

Many students drop out of high school because they are bored. They don't feel challenged. Even at the collegiate level, they have problems with having to take courses in so many fields where there is little to no interest. The program Excellence for All consolidates the high school career from four years to two. It's something your administrative team needs to become familiarized. Investigate which students could benefit from this program.

I don't want to see this program only being provided for AP, gifted and talented students. In so many schools, student placement in these programs is based on test scores or teacher recommendations. More African American students could handle AP, gifted and talented classes, but because they may have done poorly on a test, they don't get referred. More Black students would be in advanced classes if the teachers were not suffering from racism, classism, and low expectations.

We could increase the number of Black students in AP, gifted and talented classes, as well as the Excellence for All program, if we move beyond individualism, i.e., only one student participates, and refer a cooperative group of students. So I'm recommending Excellence for All, but for a minimum of five boys at a time.

Support Programs

I also want to acknowledge the excellent work of the AVID program. AVID (which stands for Advancement Via Individual Determination) is concerned about the disproportionate number of children of color who are not placed in AP, gifted, and talented classes. I have enjoyed working with them. They found an even greater disparity in the shortage of African American males in AP, gifted and talented classes. AVID has found that the participation of Black males in these programs can be increased if Black male instructors are provided.

Isn't that interesting? All we have to do to increase the academic success of African American males is to provide them with an African

American male Master Teacher. AVID found that Black boys have a great desire to participate in AP, gifted and talented classes if there are more Black male students in the class and if they are taught by Black male teachers.

Drs. Thomas S. Dee and Byron L. Daniels found that when you provide Black students with African American teachers, their test scores improve. They not only found this to be true based on grade, but it was also true based on gender. When you provide African American males with an African American male teacher, there's a quantitative increase in GPA, test scores, and overall academic achievement. [41]

It is no longer acceptable to say that you don't know where to find African American teachers. I often hear this comment from principals and administrators. We must accept the responsibility and acknowledge the research that African American male students need more African American male teachers.

I encourage you to contact the excellent program, Call Me MISTER ("MISTER" stands for Mentors Instructing Students Toward Effective Role Models). It's now in about 17 states and hopefully your state is one of them or will be next. Colleges are providing grants, scholarships, and consultants to mentor young African American males who are pursuing a degree in education. I have enjoyed mentoring MISTER students.

It always helps when a White scholar or individual in a significant position also acknowledges the importance of recruiting more African American male teachers. I commend the U.S. Secretary of Education, Arne Duncan, who has gone on record and stated that there needs to be an initiative to increase the number of African American male teachers. This is a very sensitive subject, especially when I stand before mostly White female teachers who think I am trying to take away their jobs. First, I think we just need to acknowledge that race and gender are important. Second, if you are an effective White female teacher, then we want you to continue doing what you've been doing in the classroom. Still, you can enhance your effectiveness by inviting on a weekly or monthly basis African American male mentors to interact with your boys. I also encourage you to expose your boys to the Children's Defense Fund Freedom Schools. They have a large number of male teachers who are committed to empowering our youth. It is an excellent program.

AFRICENTRIC CURRICULUM

We could change the culture for Black males if we gave them a curriculum that was truthful. We could change the culture if we gave them their history 9 months and not just February. If Black males knew their history they would not associate being smart with acting white. It would reduce fighting, suspensions and the use of the B and N words. Black boys need to know their ancestors built the first civilization. They need to know

Chapter 24: Miscellaneous Solutions

more history before 1620 than afterwards. There are numerous Africentric schools that have improved their test scores over 30% by using an Africentric curriculum. One of the most popular curricula is SETCLAE (Self-Esteem Through Culture Leads to Academic Excellence)

INTERNSHIPS

Every Black male needs to be given an internship. Every Black male should be exposed to more than their neighborhoods. They need to be exposed to affluence. I love the internship Your Doctors DC. High school students spend four years in Washington DC shadowing doctors. We need to ask every Black male what are your career aspirations? We then need to find those institutions and negotiate an internship. We could drastically reduce suspensions and the dropout rate with internships.

Other After-School Activities

In the last chapter, we discussed using an after-school program for leadership development activities. The after-school program can include other activities as you deem necessary for the growth and development of your boys. For example:

- Basketball
- Hip hop studio, where boys can write and record their rap lyrics
- Debate club, where boys can study, discuss, and write about different sides of issues (based on pros and cons, today versus yesterday, individual opinions versus society's attitudes, etc.) and develop critical thinking and language arts skills
- Business club, where they fine-tune their business plan or stock market portfolio
- Real estate committee, where they identify properties that need to be acquired and rehabbed
- Computer lab

Whatever programs you and the boys want to consider is fair game for the after school program. After chess, martial arts, and rites of passage, what activities would your boys like?

As I've mentioned, the greatest problem our boys face is not biology, chemistry, or physics, algebra, geometry, or trigonometry. It's the trip to and from home and school. The after school program reduces some of the hours our boys are being challenged by the street and gangs. In addition, transportation home should be provided to ensure their safety and circumvent the gang problem.

Mission Statements and Creeds

When I visit a school, all I have to do is look in the main corridor to get a very good idea of the culture and what the principal, administrative team, and staff think of their students. Next, I look for the school's mission statement, and I don't mean one that's filed away in a cabinet or security vault, never to be seen or read again. I'm looking for a mission statement or creed that is visible in the main corridor, every classroom, the gym, the library, the cafeteria, and it is read on a daily basis. Take for example the following creed for Urban Prep in Chicago.

Urban Prep Creed:
We believe.
We are the young men of Urban Prep.
We are college bound.
We are exceptional—not because we say it, but because we work hard at it.
We will not falter in the face of any obstacle placed before us.
We are dedicated, committed and focused.
We never succumb to mediocrity, uncertainty or fear.
We never fail because we never give up.
We make no excuses.
We choose to live life honestly, nonviolently and honorably.
We respect ourselves and, in doing so, respect all people.
We have a future for which we are accountable.
We have a responsibility to our families, community and world.
We are our brothers' keepers.
We believe in ourselves.
We believe in each other.
We believe in Urban Prep.
We BELIEVE.

That mission statement created a culture in the school where there is now a 100 percent success rate of their graduates being accepted into four-year colleges. This school is in the poorest neighborhood of Chicago. The other public schools in the neighborhood have an average graduation rate of 35 percent; less than 10 percent of their Black males are accepted into four-year colleges.

We must change school culture for Black males. Following are more creeds that I've collected over the years.

I am an honor roll student.
I have a great future.
I can be whatever I want.
I am good in science and sports, math and music, reading and rap.
I respect my teachers. They will help me achieve.

We believe all students *will* learn, not can learn. I am the teacher my students have been waiting for.

Chapter 24: Miscellaneous Solutions

We are not concerned about our students' race, gender, income, or parental educational achievement.

We believe high expectations, good classroom management, greater time on task, differentiated instruction, and using test data to drive instruction produces academic excellence.

I am the Black man.
Some know me as Malcolm, some know me as Martin.
I am the Black man, the original man.
I am spiritually strong, mentally strong, and physically strong.
I am the Black man, the original man.
I respect my elders. I respect my sisters. I respect my brothers. I respect my teachers.
I am the Black man, the original man.

In my book, There is Nothing Wrong with Black Students, we observed over 3000 plus schools who are successfully educating African American students. Many of them have a brief staff meeting daily to keep each other informed and inspired. I encourage you to do the same. Others also have their staff to greet the students as they enter the school. We must make our students feel welcomed and important.

We will now move to the conclusion.

Chapter 25: Conclusion

Are you satisfied with the academic performance of your African American male students?

Are you satisfied with their GPA and reading scores?

Are you satisfied with the percent of African American males in special education, remedial reading, or retained?

Are you satisfied with the percent of African American males who are suspended and dropping out?

Would you like to do more?

Do you think you could do better?

Do you think your staff and peers could do better?

The problem is far deeper than test scores. The problem is academic, social and emotional. Throughout this book, I have attempted to show that the problem facing Black boys is much more than just a quantitative problem. We must change school culture. The staff must share the mission, values, and creed of the school. The staff must be convinced that all Black males *will* learn, regardless of race, gender, income, or the educational background of the parent.

We must go into the world of Black males and connect Black male culture with school culture. One of the reasons for this schism has been the failure of schools to address the major issues, needs, and challenges facing African American males.

We must be willing to disaggregate the scores by race and gender. We must be willing to disaggregate the solutions by race and gender.

In some schools, only five percent of the student population is African American male. In others, it's 50 percent. Some solutions provided in this book are easier to implement in one environment than another.

In addition, the Black community is not monolithic. Some Black males attend school in affluent suburbs. Others attend school in the inner city and some Black males attend school in moderate-income urban or suburban communities. In my dedication, while the three males had different demographics they all were behind in reading and had been retained.

To change school culture for boys, our mantra has been, "20-25 boys, three/four years at a time with master teachers" We should not overwhelm ourselves and our resources by trying to solve the problem for 500 to 1,000 Black males. While that would be my desire, I don't want that to be an excuse for inertia.

Chapter 25: Conclusion

Throughout this book, I've given you almost 100 solutions, but if you can only implement 14, I recommend the following:

1. Identify your most challenging 20-25 Black male students in kindergarten and third grade, and have them loop with a Master Teacher, preferably an African American male teacher. Do the same in sixth and ninth grade with four Master Teachers, each one teaching three/four years each of language arts, math, science, and social studies.
2. Create cooperative learning groups for each class.
3. Offer a weekly or monthly convocation with a motivational speaker, with an emphasis on STEM.
4. Place a moratorium on special education placements unless the problem is a lack of hearing, sight, or limb. Empower your pre-referral intervention team to work with the classroom teachers referring students on mainstreaming strategies. Place a moratorium on out-of-school suspensions. Suspensions should only be in-school. Have your team work with those teachers who have a high referral of suspensions.
5. Give your boys the selection of books titled *Best Books for Boys.* Give prizes to the group that has read, spoken about, and written about the most books.
6. Require all boys to develop a business plan and understand the stock market. Give prizes to the group that performs the best. Have the boys create businesses in your school in which they profit.
7. Implement a mandatory after school program that includes leadership development, chess, martial arts, and rites of passage.
8. Provide a mentor to as many boys as possible.
9. Offer as many single-gender classrooms as possible.
10. Require a business dress uniform and gym shoes cannot be worn.
11. Give every Black male a college application to complete and a trip to Morehouse College.
12. Hold academic assemblies (Nguzo Saba) with an emphasis on "we," not "I," and give prizes to the cooperative groups who have performed the best.
13. Develop an optimistic and collaborative staff. Create a teacher of the month award, monitor the teacher's lounge and have more frequent staff meetings.
14. Place your best teachers in the primary grades and monitor internal test results. We must make sure every Black male is on grade level in reading before fourth grade.

Principals must identify the 20 percent of their staff who are making 80 percent of the referrals to special education and suspension. Make it difficult for these staff members to remain in the building. This small percentage is negatively infecting the culture of your school. Principals must provide more staff development. If that is not effective, either remove these teachers from the school or reduce their involvement with African American males.

The future of Black males lies in the hands of principals. If the problem is in the principal's office, Black males have a problem. CEO principals cannot change school culture for the better. It's difficult to change school culture when a school had a different principal every year... We need superintendents to provide Black males with the best principals who will stay a minimum of four years. Can you imagine some schools lose staff from Teach for America every two years, principals every year and the remaining staff every five years?

We need principals to ensure that their staff raises expectations, bond with their students, understand their unique learning styles, give more time on task, and provide differentiated instruction.

I want to acknowledge the great work of COSEBOC, the National Education Association's Priority Schools Campaign, Everyone Graduates Center at Johns Hopkins University, the Montgomery County Public Schools in Maryland, the National Center for Urban School Transformation, the Consortium on Chicago School Research, Black Star Project, Open Society and many others who understand the problem is not with Black males, their families, or neighborhoods. We must change the culture of schools and make them more conducive to maximizing the development of African American male students.

I opened this book with this question:

Are we sending our boys to college/ entrepreneurship or are we sending them to prison?

After reading this book about changing school culture for Black boys, what's your answer? Will you do what you can to improve the culture of your school?

Just like patients who want a pill for their obesity, high blood pressure, and cholesterol rather than addressing the root problem, over my almost 40-year career, schools and school districts have always wanted me to provide solutions. I have done the best I can over the years, but I've come to accept the reality. Academic solutions are ineffective without positive relationships between students and educators.

Do you like Black males?

Do you respect Black males?

Do you enjoy being in their presence?

Do you believe they can be scholars?

Are you willing to go into their world?

Are you willing to understand and respect their world?

Let's change school culture— 20-25 boys every three/ four years with a master teacher and cooperative learning groups.

Epilogue

David Boone was 14 year- old Black male when his family lost their home to gang violence. David refused to join a gang and they retaliated. David lived on the mean streets of Cleveland for over two years. He would do his homework in the heated transit station. He would sleep on benches in the afternoon because he said they don't bother you during the day. He used his book bag as a pillow. His friend would sneak him into the house in the morning when his parents left to wash up before school. During his junior year, his school nurse allowed David to stay with them. During his senior year, David stayed with his principal. David graduated from high school, the salutatorian of his class. He earned a Bill Gates scholarship. He was accepted by Princeton, Brown, Yale, Harvard and many others. He chose Harvard. In his commencement speech, he said, "me and my class will change the world!"

References

1. Toldson, Ivory and Janks Morton. "A Million Reasons There're More Black Men in College Than in Prison," *Journal of Negro Education,* Winter 2011, pp. 1-4.
2. Adams, Caralee, Erik Robelen and Nirvi Shah. "Civil Rights Data Show Retention Disparities," *Education Week,* March 6, 2012, pp. 1-18.
3. Washington, Jesse. "Blacks Struggle with 72 Percent Unwed Mothers Rate," NBCNews.com, November 7, 2010, www.nbcnews.com/id/39993685/ns/health-womens_health/#.UUsoITdqIVg/.
4. "Criminal Justice Fact Sheet, NAACP, 2012, www.naacp.org/pages/criminal-justice-fact-sheet/; *Unlocking America,* Washington, DC: JFA Institute, 2012, p. 1, www.jfa-associates.com/publications.
5. *The School Principal as Leader.* New York: Wallace Foundation, January 2013, www.wallacefoundation.org/knowledge-center/.
6. Goodwin, Bryan. "Culture, the 'Secret Sauce' of School Improvement," *Changing Schools,* Summer 2009, www.ksde.org/LinkClick.aspx?fileticket=wx170wph10%3D&tabid=4398.
7. Lewis, Shawn, et al. *A Call for Change.* Washington, DC: Council of the Great City Schools, November 2010, p. 32.
8. *State of America's Children.* Washington, DC: Children's Defense Fund, 2010, pp. G-1, G-6.
9. Ehri, Linnea, et al. "Systematic Phonics Instruction Helps Students Learn to Read: Evidence from the National Reading Panel's Meta-Analysis," *Review of Educational Research,* Fall 2001, pp. 393-447.
10. Krache, Donna. "Nation's Report Card: Writing Test Shows Gender Gap," September 17, 2012, www.schoolsofthought.blogs.cnn.com/.../2012.
11. Fletcher, Ralph J. *Boy Writers: Reclaiming Their Voices.* Portland, ME: Stenhouse Publishers, 2006, pp. 73-78.
12. "New Study Finds Big Racial Gap in Suspensions of Middle School Students," Southern Poverty Law Center, September 14, 2010, www.splcenter.org/get-informed/news/.
13. Shah, Nirvi. "Study Finds Minority Students Get Harsher Punishments," *Education Week,* October 5, 2011, www.edweek.org/ew/articles/2011/10/05/07/discipline_ep.h31.html/.
14. Johnson, Stanley. "An Interview with Dr. Jawanza Kunjufu," *Journal of African American Males in Education,* Leading Educators Series, Vol. 2, Issue 1/2, 2011, pp. 141-145.
15. "Table 1: State Graduation Data," *The Urgency of Now: The Schott 50 State Report on Black Males and Public Education.* Cambridge, MA: Schott Foundation for Public Education, 2012, www.blackboys report.org.
16. Kunjufu, Jawanza. *Reducing the Black Male Dropout Rate.* Chicago: African American Images, 2010, p. 58.
17. ibid., p. 59.
18. Hendrie, Caroline. "Alienation from High School Is Worst Among Black Males," *Education Week,* January 28, 1998, p. 1.
19. Matthews, Jamaal. "Toward a Holistic Understanding of Academic Identification." PhD dissertation, University of Michigan, 2010. http://hdl.handle.net/2027.42/77823.
20. Buck, Stuart. *Acting White.* New Haven: Yale University Press, 2011, pp. 10-11, 34-35; Fryer, Roland G. "'Acting White': The Social Price Paid by the Best and Brightest Minority Students," *Education Next,* Winter 2006, p. 56.
21. "Study Finds Black Youngsters Perform Better Than Whites in Different Learning Environments," *Journal of Blacks in Higher Education,* June 18, 2009, p. 139.

22. Delpit, Lisa. *"Multiplication Is for White People": Raising Expectations for Other People's Children.* New York: New Press, 2012. p. 154.
23. Torre, Pablo. "How (and Why) Athletes Go Broke," *Sports Illustrated,* March 23, 2009, www.sportsillustrated.cnn.com/vault/article/magazine/MAG1153364.
24. Powers, Lindsay. "African Americans Watch the Most TV (Study)," March 31, 2011, www. Hollywoodreporter.com/news/.
25. Olson, Cheryl K., et al. "Factors Correlated with Violent Video Game Use by Adolescent Boys and Girls," *Journal of Adolescent Health,* 2007, pp. 77-83; Terraso, David. "Video Game Testing Helping to Spark Computing Interest in African-American Youths," *The Whistle,* Georgia Institute of Technology, September 21, 2009.
26. Child Trends. www.blacklifecoaches.net; Burton, Nsenga. "72 Percent of African-American Children Born to Unwed Mothers," The Root, November 9, 2010, www.theroot.com/.
27. *Sexually Transmitted Disease Surveillance 2011.* Atlanta, GA: Centers for Disease Control, Division of STD Prevention, December 2012, www.cdc.gov/std/stats 11/Surv2011.pdf.
28. "HIV among African Americans," Atlanta, GA: Centers for Disease Control, February 2013, www.cdc.gov/hiv/topics.
29. Kunjufu, Jawanza. *Understanding Black Male Learning Styles.* Chicago: African American Images, 2011, pp. 29-50.
30. *Child Poverty in America.* Washington, DC: Children's Defense Fund, 2011; "Information on Poverty and Income Statistics: A Summary of 2012 Current Population Survey Data," September 12, 2012, www.aspe.hhs.gov/hsp/12/; "Poverty Data Table 3: Annual Social and Economic Supplement, Current Population Survey," Washington, DC: U.S. Census Bureau, 2011, www.census.gov/.
31. "African American Income," www.blackdemographics.com/households/african-american-imcone/.
32. Levine, Marc. "Race and Male Employment in the Wake of the Great Recession: Black Male Employment Rates in Milwaukee and the Nation's Largest Metro Areas, 2010," Working Paper, Milwaukee: University of Wisconsin-Milwaukee, Center for Economic Development, January 2012, http://www4.uwm.edu/ced/publications/.
33. Fischer, Wendi. "Educational Value of Chess," July 2006, New Horizons for Learning, Johns Hopkins School of Education, www.education. jhu. edu/PD/newhorizons/.
34. Shah, Nirvi. "At S.C. School, Behavior Is One of the Basics," *Education Week,* October 24, 2012, pp. 1-12.
35. Yee, Doris and Jacqueline Eccles. "A Comparison of Parents' and Children's Attributions for Successful and Unsuccessful Math Performances." Paper presented at APA Annual Convention, Anaheim, CA, August 30, 1983.
36. "Single-Sex vs. Coed: The Evidence," National Association for Single Sex Public Education, www.singlesexschools.org/research-singles exvscoed.htm/.
37. Abdul-Alim, "Forum Highlights Efforts to Boost Academic Achievement among Minority Males," Eagle Academy Foundation, May 15, 2012, www.eagleacademyfoundation.com/presskit_3_631602310.pdf.
38. "Urban Prep: 100 Percent of Graduates College-Bound for Second Straight Year," Huffington Post, February 7, 2011, www.huffington post.com/2011/02/16/.
39. ibid.
40. ibid.
41. Daniels, Byron L. "Academic Achievement of African-American Male Students in Relationship to African-American Male Teachers in Guilford County, North Carolina." PhD dissertation, Capella University, 2010, ISBN: 978-1-1243-9167-0; Dee, Thomas S. "Teachers, Race and Student Achievement in a Randomized Experiment," *The Review of Economics and Statistics,* February 2004, pp. 195-210.